BIBLE PLACES...

Historic
and
Geographic Highlights

3397

Compiled by
ANTOINETTE MITCHELL

Designed by
Tyyne Hakola

Published by
THE C. R. GIBSON COMPANY ● NORWALK, CONNECTICUT

the accent mark (′) is used to denote the
primary accent or chief stress in the word.

BIBLE PLACES
A DICTIONARY

A

ACELDAMA (a-cel'da-ma) A parcel of ground known as potter's field. Traditionally, since the 4th century, this site is believed to be on the southern side of the valley of Hinnom near Jerusalem. The priests bought it with the thirty pieces of silver Judas received for betraying Jesus to the Roman soldiers. It was used as a cemetery and was referred to as the "field of blood" because Judas hanged himself in it. (Matthew 27:5-8; Acts 1:19)

ACHAIA (a-cha'-ia) One of two provinces into which Greece was divided after being conquered by Caesar Augustus. Macedonia was the other. Corinth was the capital of Achaia. Paul

The Province of Achaia

Judas returned the thirty pieces of silver and hanged himself.   MATTHEW 27: 3-8

spent one and a half years in this area while on his missionary journey, before leaving for Ephesus. (Acts 18:1-18)

ACHMETHA (a-ch'-me-tha) A city in the province of Medes. Here a document was found that verified the decree given by Cyrus that the temple should be rebuilt in Jerusalem. (Ezra 6:2) It was probably the summer residence of the Persian kings.

ACHOR A valley near Jericho forming the northern boundary of Judah. (Joshua 15:7) Joshua and all Israel took Achan, his family and all his possessions into the valley of Achor. Here they stoned them to death, because he kept part of the spoils of Jericho against the Lord's commandment to destroy everything but silver, gold, brass and iron. (Joshua 7:24-26)

AENON A locality of many springs near Salem in the Jordan valley. John the Baptist baptized here because there was plenty of water. (John 3:23)

AI (in Genesis Hai) Abram built an altar and sojourned in Canaan near Ai, which was east of Bethel, after he had been told by God to leave Haran. (Genesis 12:2-8) After one defeat at Ai, caused by the sin of Achan, Joshua, with a mighty army, finally overcame and destroyed the city. (Joshua Ch. 7&8) It was later rebuilt. (Ezra 2:28)

AJALON (a'ja-lon) A city of Dan assigned as a Levitical city. (Joshua 19:42; 21:24) It was with reference to the valley named after this town that Joshua said "Sun stand thou still upon Gibeon; and thou, moon, in the valley of Ajalon." The sun stood still and the moon stayed in its position until the Israelites avenged themselves upon their enemy, the Amorites. (Joshua 10:12-14)

ALEXANDRIA (al-ex-an'-dria) A port city founded by Alexander the Great in 332 B.C. on the north coast of Egypt on the Mediterranean Sea. It was the main port for the export of cargo from Egypt to Rome. The city was inhabited by many nationalities, each occupying a different section. The Jews resided in the northern section and had their own synagogue. (Acts 6:9) Apollos, a follower of the teachings of John the Baptist, was a native of Alexandria. He became a teacher of Christianity, having been instructed by Aquila and Priscilla. (Acts 18:24-26)

ANATHOTH A city in the territory of Benjamin, assigned to the priests. (Joshua 21:18; I Chronicles 6:60) It was the birthplace of the prophet Jeremiah, (Jeremiah 1:1) and the home of Abiathar, the high priest. (I Kings 2:26) The Jews returning from the Babylonian exile repopulated Anathoth. (Ezra 2:23) It was situated a short distance northeast of Jerusalem on a hill overlooking the Jordan Valley.

ANTIOCH A city in Syria founded about 300 B.C. It was situated on the southern side of the Orontes River about 20 miles in from the sea. Antioch was the third largest city in the Roman Empire, a city of wealth, culture and luxury. Both Jews and Gentiles lived here. Christians fleeing persecution after the stoning of Stephen came to Antioch and preached the Gospel. Later Barnabas was sent to help with this work, and for the first time the disciples of Christ were called Christians. (Acts 11:19-26) Paul's first and second missionary journeys were started from Antioch. (Acts 13:2; 15:35-36)

ANTIOCH OF PISIDIA A town in Asia minor. Paul and Barnabas visited here on their first missionary journey and preached in the synagogue. They were driven out of the city by unbelieving Jews. (Acts 13:14-52; 14:19-21; II Timothy 3:11)

Paul's first and second missionary journeys
See large map on page 68 for more detail on Paul's missionary journeys.

APPIAN WAY   A road on which Paul, as a prisoner, walked on his way to Rome. (Acts 28:15)

ARABIA   A desert area forming a peninsula, bounded by the Red Sea, the Persian Gulf and the Arabian Sea. Midian was a region in Arabia. In Genesis the Arab tribes came into contact with the Hebrews when Joseph was sold to the Midianites for 20 pieces of silver. (Genesis 37:28,36)   The Lord delivered the Israelites into the hands of the Midianites.   (Judges 6)   Solomon bought silver and gold from the Arabs. (II Chronicles 9:14)   Arabians brought tribute to Jehoshaphat.   (II Chronicles 17:11) They plundered Jerusalem during the realm of Jehoram, (II Chronicles 21:16) and were later defeated by Uzziah.   (II Chronicles 26:7)   Paul stayed in Arabia before beginning his apostolic work.   (Galatians 1:17)

ARAD   A town in southern Palestine not far from Mount Hor. The king of Arad fought against Israel when they were at Mount Hor and took some of them as prisoners.   (Numbers 21:1)   Later, under Joshua, the Lord delivered the king of Arad to Israel and they destroyed the people.   (Joshua 12:14)

ARARAT (ar'a-rat)   Noah's ark rested on Mount Ararat and remained there seven months while the flood waters receded.   Noah released a dove which came back with an olive leaf and Noah knew the land was dry.   (Genesis 8:4)   Ararat is a mountain range midway between the Black Sea and the Caspian Sea in Armenia. It is a double coned mountain with peaks about 7 miles apart. One peak is about 17,000 ft. high and the other about 13,000 ft. Tradition implies the ark rested on the southern side of the loftiest peak.

AREOPAGUS (ar·e·op′·a·gus) A hill in Athens consecrated to the Greek god of war, Ares. The supreme court of Athens met on Areopagus hill. It was here that Paul pleaded the cause of Christianity before the philosophers of the Epicureans and the Stoics, who refused to believe in the resur‑rection of the dead. (Acts 17:18‑33) There were, however, some who believed, including Areopagite, Dionysius and a woman called Damaris. (Acts 17:34)

Noah's sacrifice and God's promise
GENESIS 8: 15‑9: 17

ARIMATHAEA (ar·i·ma·thae′·a) Joseph, a Jew and secret disciple of Jesus, came from here. He asked Pilate for the body of Jesus and buried Him in his own sepulcher. Arimathaea was located west of Jerusalem. (Matthew 27:57‑60; Mark 15:43‑46; Luke 23:51‑53; John 19:38‑42)

AROER (ar′·o·er) A town on the north bank of the Arnon River, west of the Dead Sea. It was in the Amorite kingdom (Deuteronomy 2:36; 3:12) ruled by King Sihon. (Joshua 12:2) Aroer was allotted to the tribe of Reuben, (Joshua 13:16) and

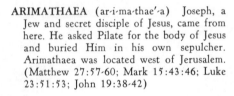

Paul talking to philosophers

was occupied by Gadites. (Numbers 32:34) It fell into the hands of King Hazael of Assyria during the reign of Jehu. (II Kings 10:33)

ASHDOD (in N. T. Azotus) One of the five principal cities of the Philistines. Together with Gaza, Gath, Ekron and Ashkelon it formed the Philistine Pentapolis. Ashdod was conquered by the Hebrews under Joshua, (Joshua 11:22) and was assigned to the tribe of Judah. (Joshua 15:46‑47) It was the seat of worship of the god Dagon. The Philistines carried the ark of God here and placed it in the temple of Dagon after seizing it at Ebenezer. Disaster fell upon the people and the ark was transferred to Gath. (I Samuel 5:1‑8) King Uzziah warred against the Philistines and broke down the walls of Ashdod. (II Chronicles 26:6) Sargon, king of Assyria, sent Tartan against it and took the city. (Isaiah 20:1) Inhabitants of this city opposed the rebuilding of the walls of Jerusalem. (Nehemiah 4:7-8) Nehemiah protested when Israelite men married women of Ashdod and raised children who could not speak Hebrew. (Nehemiah 13:23-25) Ashdod was situated on a hill a short distance from the Great Sea on the caravan route, a position of importance.

ASHER The territory assigned to the tribe of Asher was about 60 miles in length in the northwestern part of Palestine, bordering on the shores of the Mediterranean Sea. (Joshua 19:24-31) At the time of the Exodus this tribe ranked ninth in population. (Numbers 1:40-41) Tyre and Sidon were cities in this area, however, the Canaanites were never expelled from all of the plain area along the seacoast. (Judges 1:31)

ASHKELON (ash'-ke-lon) A principal city in Philistia located about 12 miles from Gaza near the Great Sea. It was taken by Judah in the time of the Judges (Judges 1:18) but later restored to its old rulers. (I Samuel 6:17) Ashkelon was the birth-place of Herod the Great and the residence of his sister Salome. David mentions this city in his lament over the death of Saul and Jonathan. (II Samuel 1:20)

ASHTAROTH (ash'-to-roth) A town in Bashan. It was inhabited by giants. Og, king of Bashan, a giant, was overthrown by the Israelites. (Deuteronomy 1:4; Joshua 9:10) Ashtaroth was given to Machir, son of Manasseh, but became a Levitical city inhabited by the children of Gershom. (I Chronicles 6:71) Uzzia, one of David's warriors came from this city. (I Chronicles 11:44)

ASIA In New Testament time, Asia was a province within the Roman Empire. It was located on the Aegean Sea. Ephesus was its capital. Scripture uses the name Asia in a re-stricted sense to refer to a separate province rather than to the whole conti-nent, also naming Phrygia, Mysia, Caria and Lydia as separate provinces. (Acts 2:9; 6:9; 19:26)

★ Denotes "Seven Churches" of Asia (REV. 1-3)

ASSYRIA It was founded before 2,000 B.C. by colonists from Babylon. The inhabitants were closely associated with Babylon, either in conflict with or subject to them, until about 1300 B.C. when Shalmaneser I and his son Tukulti-Ninurta threw off the yoke of Babylon and ruled the entire Euphrates valley. In subsequent years Assyria declined until it was once again made a powerful nation by Tiglath-pileser I (1120-1100). During the time of David and Solomon it again declined in power. From 885 to

607 B.C. it was once more restored to power and ruled by 10 kings. The northern kingdom of Israel was taken into captivity by the Assyrians under King Tiglath-pileser III in 734 B.C., (II Kings 17:5-6) and during the reign of Sargon (722-705) Samaria was destroyed and Israel's captivity was completed. In 605 B.C. it was overthrown by the Neo-Babylonian Empire. Assyria was referred to as the extensive area conquered and ruled by the Assyrians in the Euphrates valley. Its capital was Nineveh. The kings and its people were cruel and ruthless warriors. They deported the Israelites to other lands in order to destroy their nationalism and culture and thus make them more easily subject to them.

ATACH (a'-thach)   A city in Judah to which David sent part of the spoils of Ziklag which he recovered from the Amalekites. (I Samuel 30:30)

ATHENS   The capital city of Greece. It was a cultural center of philosophy, literature, science and art. The city was wholly given to idolatry. Paul had difficulty convincing the people of the Christian doctrine. (Acts 17:15-34) He did not establish a church here. It was in Athens that Paul found the altar dedicated to the unknown god. (Acts 17:23)

David slays Goliath   I SAMUEL 17: 40-54

AZEKAH (a-ze'-kah)   A fortified city in Judah (Jeremiah 34:7) with villages on the outskirts of the city. (Nehemiah 11:30) Here five Amorite kings were killed by hailstones. (Joshua 10:10-11) Goliath and the Philistines encamped near this city before the battle between David and Goliath. (I Samuel 17:1) It was fortified by Rehoboam, (II Chronicles 11:9) and the fort was still standing at the time of the Babylonian invasion. (Jeremiah 34:7)

B

BABEL   About one hundred years after the flood, the tower of Babel was erected in the plain of Shinar by the descendants of Noah. Prompted by pride and the desire to make a name for themselves, they planned a tower made of bricks and slime that would reach to the heavens. Their plans were never fully carried out for God confused their language so they could not understand one another. They were scattered abroad on the whole face of the earth. (Genesis 11:3-9) Babel was the first kingdom of Nimrod, the mighty warrior, and descendant of Cush. (Genesis 10:10) Babel later became Babylon.

Tower of Babel
GENESIS 11: 3-9

BABYLON The capital city of the Babylonian Empire. It was founded by the descendants of Nimrod and his followers. (Genesis 8:10) At first it was called Babel but after the confusion of tongues and the scattering of the people it became Babylon. (Genesis 11:1-9) It was a political and religious center under King Hammurabi and reached the peak of its glory in the 6th century B.C. when Nebuchadnezzar made it his capital. The city was surrounded by two walls between which were planted gardens, orchards and fields. (Jeremiah 51:58) The walls had 25 gates on each of the four sides of the city, and streets ran at right angles to the walls from these gates, dividing it into squares. The Euphrates River flowed through the city. The many prophesies concerning Babylon were fulfilled. It fell in 539 B.C. to Cyrus, king of Persia. After this it declined and became a desert never to be revived. (Jeremiah 50 and 51; Isaiah 13; 14: 1-23; 21:1-10; 47:1-3)

BABYLONIA An area in western Asia sometimes called Shinar, (Genesis 10:10; 11:2; Isaiah 11:11) and also the land of the Chaldeans. (Jeremiah 24:5; 25:12; Ezekiel 12:13) It was bounded on the north by Mesopotamia, on the east by Elam,

The Babylonian Empire

9

on the south by the Persian Gulf and the west by the Arabian desert. After 1260 B.C. Assyria made Babylonia a subject nation. Its independence was again secured in 625 B.C. and it soon became the great Neo-Babylonian Empire under King Nabopolassar. It was under his son, Nebuchadnezzar that the empire reached its greatest expanse of territory. During his rule Jerusalem was captured and destroyed and the people of Judah were carried into captivity. (II Kings 24 and 25; II Chronicles 36:5-21; Jeremiah 39 and 52) In 539 B.C. Cyrus, the Persian king, entered Babylonia and terminated the empire.

BASHAN An area east of the Jordan River. It was a fertile area noted for its fine breed of cattle. (Ezekiel 39:18; Psalms 22:12; Jeremiah 50:19) The cities in Bashan were many and fenced with high walls. (Deuteronomy 3:4-5; I Kings 4:13) The principal cities were Ashtaroth, (Deuteronomy 1:4) Edrei, (Deuteronomy 1:4) Golan, (Deuteronomy 4:43) and Salchah (Deuteronomy 3:10) It contained Argob, famous for its 60 high walled cities. (Deuteronomy 3:4-5) The inhabitants of Bashan were of very large stature and referred to as Rephaim. (Genesis 14:5) King Og, a giant, was defeated by the Israelites and slain. (Numbers 21:33-35; Deuteronomy 1:4; 3:1-4; 29:7) Bashan was then assigned to the half tribe of Manasseh. (Deut. 3:13)

BEERSHEBA (beer-she'ba) A place of seven wells where Abraham, Isaac and Jacob dwelt much of the time. It was in the southernmost part of Canaan, halfway between the Great Sea and the Salt Sea. Abraham and Abimelech made a covenant at the well not to do harm to one another and Abraham planted a grove and called it Beersheba. (Genesis 21:21-34) The Philistines filled the well, but when Isaac came to those parts, he had it opened and once again called it Beersheba. Here he made a pact with the king of Gerar, just as his father had done. (Genesis 26:27-33) It was from here that Jacob set out to Haran to find a wife. (Genesis 28:10) Later the area became a city of Judah occupied by the sons of Simeon. (I Chronicles 4:28) Samuel's sons were judges in Beersheba. (I Samuel 8:2) Elijah stopped here when he fled from Jezebel. (I Kings 19:3) It was occupied by sons of Judah after the captivity. (Nehemiah 11:27-30)

BENJAMIN The tribe of Benjamin was assigned the land between that of Judah to the south, Ephraim to the north, with the Jordan River as its eastern boundary. The territory of Benjamin contained the cities of Bethel, Jericho, Gibeon and Mizpeh among others of lesser importance. (Joshua 18:11-28) During the first census Benjamin was one of the smaller tribes with 35,000 males over twenty years old. (Numbers 1:36-37)

BEREA (be-re'a) A Macedonian city where Paul preached on his first missionary journey. Many Jews became followers of the Gospel, and were diligent in searching the Scriptures daily. (Acts 17:10-12)

BETHABARA (beth-ab'a-ra) An important crossing of the Jordan River. It was here that John gave testimony of Christ and baptized. (John 1:19-28)

BETHANY A small town on the eastern slope of the Mount of Olives about two miles from Jerusalem. (Luke 19:29) Jesus often visited here at the home of Lazarus and his sisters Mary and Martha. He also visited at the home of Simon, the Leper, where He was anointed with oil. (Matthew 26:6-13; Mark 11:1,11; 14:3-9) Jesus raised Lazarus from the dead in Bethany. (John 11:1-46) It was near the town that Jesus ascended into heaven. (Luke 24:50-51)

Martha was concerned about much serving while Mary listened to Jesus. LUKE 10: 38-42

BETHEL Abraham first visited Bethel after leaving Ur. He built an altar and prayed unto the Lord. (Genesis 12:8) Both he and Lot returned here after leaving Egypt. This was before they separated when Lot went to Sodom. (Genesis 13:3-12) It was here that Jacob dreamed of the ladder reaching to heaven. (Genesis 28:11-19) Bethel was formerly called Luz, (Genesis 28:19; Judges 1:23) and was situated in Canaan about twelve miles north of Jerusalem. It was allotted to the children of Benjamin who failed to take it from the inhabitants. Later it was occupied by the sons of Joseph. (Judges 1:22-26) Samuel judged the Israelites from Bethel as well as from Gilgal and Mizpeh. (I Samuel 7:16) Jeroboam, scheming to keep the allegiance of his people, set up a golden calf at Bethel and Dan for them to worship. (I Kings 12:26-29) Josiah removed these idols and restored the true worship of Jehovah. (II Kings 23:15-20) Elijah and Elisha passed through Bethel. Later while here, Elisha was mocked by youths who in turn

Jacob's dream GENESIS 28: 10-17

were attacked by bears. (II Kings 2:1-3; 2:23-24) The people returning from captivity again occupied Bethel. (Ezra 2:28; Nehemiah 11:31) The prophets denounced it for its idolatry. (Jeremiah 48:13; Hosea 10:15; Amos 3:14; 4:4-6;5:5-6)

BETHESDA A pool in Jerusalem near the sheep gate with healing qualities. It had five porches on which the invalids waited for their turn to enter the pool to be healed. (John 5:2-4) Jesus healed a man on the Sabbath who had been lame for 38 years. (John 5:5-9)

BETHLEHEM Best known as the town where Jesus was born. Joseph and Mary traveled to Bethlehem, the city of David, to be taxed, and while they were here Jesus was born of Mary in a stable. (Matthew 2:1; Luke 2:1-7) It was a town in the hill country of Judah about five miles south of Jerusalem. It existed as early as the time of Jacob and was originally called Ephrath. Rachel died and was buried near here. (Genesis 35:15-18) It was the residence of Elimelech, husband of Naomi, (Ruth 1:1) and Boaz in whose fields Ruth gleaned of the harvest. (Ruth ch. 2) David was born here and here Samuel anointed him as the future king of Israel.

The Nativity
LUKE 2: 1-20

(I Samuel 16:4-13) It was reinhabited after the captivity. (Ezra 2:21) After the birth of Jesus, Magi came to Bethlehem to worship Him and Herod ordered all male babies to be slain. (Matthew 2:1-18)

BETHPEOR (beth-pe'-or) A town near Mount Pisgah, east of the Jordan River. In the valley near here was the last stopping place of the children of Israel east of the Jordan. (Deuteronomy 3:27-29) In this valley Moses rehearsed the laws and judgments to the people. (Deuteronomy 4:44-46) Here he was told by God that he would not enter the promised land. He died and was buried in this valley. (Deuteronomy 34:1-6)

BETHPHAGE (beth'pha-ge) A village near Bethany, not far from Jerusalem, from whence Jesus sent the two disciples to find the colt on which He rode into Jerusalem. (Matthew 21:1; Mark 11:1; Luke 19:29)

BETHSAIDA (beth-sai'-da) A fishing village in Galilee where Philip, Andrew and Peter lived. (John 1:44) It was located on the northeast end of the Sea of Galilee. Jesus came here after hearing about the death of John the Baptist. From here He went to a grassy area nearby followed by a multitude. After speaking to them, He miraculously fed five thousand people with five loaves of bread and two fishes. (Matthew 14:13-21;

Jesus calls His disciples. MATTHEW 4: 18-22

Mark 6:30-45; Luke 9:10-17; John 6:1-14) Jesus upbraided the inhabitants of Bethsaida for not accepting His teachings. (Luke 10:11-14)

BETHSHEAN (beth-she'-an) A city in the Jezreel Valley close to the Jordan River. The inhabitants were strengthened by the use of chariots made of iron. (Joshua 17:16) It was allotted to the Manassites who failed to drive out the Canaanites, but did succeed in making them pay tribute. (Joshua 17:11-13) At the battle of Gilboa, when Saul and his three sons were killed, the inhabitants of Bethshean must have been in alliance with the Philistines for the bodies of Saul and his sons were fastened to its walls. (I Samuel 31:10-12; II Samuel 21:12-14) During the reign of Solomon it was a district under Baana. (I Kings 4:12)

BETHSHEMESH (beth-she'-mesh) A city in the territory of Judah given to the children of Aaron. (Joshua 21:16, 15-10; I Chronicles 6:59) When the ark of the Lord brought disaster to the Philistines they brought it to Bethshemesh to rid themselves of it. (I Samuel 6:9-15) People of this city looked into the ark and as a result over fifty thousand men were slain, presumably from a plague. (I Samuel 6:19-21) It was one of the cities that provided food for Solomon and his household. (I Kings 4:7-9) Here Jehoash, king of Israel defeated Amaziah, king of Judah. (II Kings 14:11-13; II Chronicles 25:21-23) Later the Philistines took it from King Ahaz. (II Chronicles 28:18)

BITHYNIA (bi-thy'n-ia) A province in the northwestern part of Asia Minor. When Paul was in Asia he was persuaded not to enter here. (Acts 16:7) The Gospel was carried here by other means since Christians living in Bithynia were included in the First Epistle of Peter. (I Peter 1:1)

C

CAESAREA (caes-a-re'a) Caesarea of Palestine was a city situated on the coast of the Mediterranean Sea in Palestine, built by Herod the Great and named for Caesar Augustus. After Saul was converted and preached in the name of Jesus, Grecians threatened his life. For safety the Christian brethren brought him to Caesarea from whence he sailed to Tarsus. (Acts 9:29-30) The Gospel was preached here by Philip, (Acts 8:40) and Paul stayed with him awhile. (Acts 21:8) Cornelius, the centurion to whom Peter came and preached resided here. (Acts 10:1-18) Paul twice revisited Caesarea, (Acts 18:22; 21:8) and later was taken here as a prisoner to be heard by Felix. (Acts 23:23,33) He was put on trial before Festus and Agrippa. Agrippa heard his testimony and said "Almost thou persuadest me to be a Christian." (Acts Ch. 25 and 26) From here Paul began his journey by boat to Rome. (Acts 27:1)

Peter preaches Christ in the house of Cornelius.

ACTS 10: 34-43

13

CAESAREA PHILIPPI A city in the northern part of Palestine at the main source of the Jordan River. Not to be confused with Caesarea of Palestine. Here Jesus asked His disciples "whom do men say that I am?" Peter confessed "Thou art the Christ." (Matthew 16:13-16; Mark 8:27-30)

CALVARY (cal'-va-ry) (skull) The place where Jesus was crucified, (Luke 23:33) referred to as Golgotha. (Matthew 27:33; John 19:17) It was outside the city walls of Jerusalem, a prominent place, perhaps near the highway. (Mark 15:40; Luke 23:49; Matthew 27:39)

CANA A village in Galilee. Here at the marriage feast, Jesus performed His first miracle by changing water to wine. (John 2:1-11) He also healed the nobleman's son. (John 4:46-54) Nathanael was of Cana. (John 21:2)

CANAAN The Holy Land, also called Palestine. Canaan, son of Ham and his descendants settled here and gave their name to this area, which at first comprised the lowlands along the coast of the Great Sea. It had Sidon to the north and Gaza to the south. (Genesis 10:6,15, 19) Later it extended to the Jordan River. (Numbers 13:29) Abram entered Canaan after he, Sari, his wife, and Lot left Haran when God called him and promised to make of him a great nation. (Genesis 12:1-6) When Lot chose to go to Sodom, Abram remained in Canaan. (Genesis 13:12) God promised Canaan to Abram and his descendants as an everlasting possession. (Genesis 12:1; 15:18;17:8) After spending 40 years in the wilderness, Moses sent spies into Canaan to look over the land. (Numbers 13:1-20) Joshua and Caleb were the only ones to bring back a good report. (Numbers 13:21 to 14:10) The Canaanites were a wicked people and God told the Israelites to exterminate them. This was not fully carried out. The territory was distributed among nine tribes of Israel: namely Judah, Joseph, Benjamin, Simeon, Zebulun, Issachar, Asher, Naphtali and Dan. Land east of Jordan had already been given to Reuben, Gad and half Manasseh. Levi did not participate in the distribution, but received certain designated cities in which they should dwell.

Speaking to His mother, Jesus said: "Woman, behold thy son."   JOHN 19: 26

Caleb and Joshua bring back a good report from the land of Canaan.   NUMBERS 14: 6-10

CAPERNAUM (ca-per'na-um) A city in Galilee on the northwest side of the Sea of

Matthew was a tax collector before Jesus called him as a disciple. MATTHEW 9: 9

Galilee. (Matthew 4:13; John 6:24) Jesus frequently came here and taught in the synagogue. (Mark 1:21; Luke 4:31; John 6:59) He came so often that it became known as His home. (Mark 2:1) Here He chose Matthew, who was gathering taxes, to be His follower. (Matthew 9:9) It was the home town of Simon Peter and Andrew — probably where Jesus told them He would make them fishers of men. (Mark 1:16-17) Jesus worked many miracles in Capernaum. He healed the centurion's servant, (Matthew 8:5-13; Luke 7:1-10) healed Peter's mother-in-law, (Matthew 8:14-15; Mark 1:30-31; Luke 4:38-39) the man sick of the palsy, (Matthew 9:1-8; Mark 2:1-12; Luke 5:18-26) and cleansed the man of the unclean spirit. (Luke 4:33-35) At Capernaum the disciples disputed as to which should be the greatest and Jesus took a child, put him in their midst and taught them. (Mark 9:33-37) Here in the synagogue Jesus spoke the discourse on the bread of life. (John 6:1-59) Capernaum is not mentioned in the O. T. Jesus reproved the people of Capernaum because they did not accept His teachings. (Matthew 11:23,24)

CAPPADOCIA (cap-pa-do'ci-a) A province in Asia Minor, east of Lycaonia. Some of its people were present on the day of Pentecost. (Acts 2:9) Peter addressed his first Epistle to the Christians who resided here. (I Peter 1:1)

CARMEL (car'mel) A range of hills in northern Palestine. They were about fifteen miles long reaching from the Mediterranean southeastward and connected by smaller hills with the mountains in central Palestine. Some parts are 1,742 feet high but as they approach the sea they drop to 556 feet. It is believed that they were cultivated to the summit with orchards and gardens. They fell within the territory of the tribe of Ashur. (Joshua 19:26) On top of Mount Carmel, Elijah proved the Lord God of Abraham to be the true God and Baal false. (I Kings 18:17-40) From here Elijah's servants saw the clouds that brought rain

In answer to Elijah's prayer the Lord sends fire from heaven. I KINGS 18: 17-40

to end the drought. (I Kings 18:41-45) Here Elisha received the Shunammite woman whose son he restored to life. (II Kings 4:25)

CHALDEA (Chal-de'a) Originally it referred to a small territory at the head of the Persian Gulf. Later practically the entire area comprising the empire was referred to as Chaldea. The Chaldean cities mentioned in the Bible are Ur, Erech, Babylon and Cuth. King Nebuchadnezzar asked the Chaldeans to interpret his dream which implies there were astrologers, scientists and magicians among the people. (Daniel 2:2-12)

CHERITH (che'-rith) A brook near the Jordan River where God told Elijah to hide himself after he predicted the drought to Ahab. Ravens fed him and he drank of the brook. (I Kings 17:1-7)

CHINNERETH (chin'ne-reth) or Cinneroth (I Kings 15:20) In the N. T. it was called the lake of Gennesaret. (Luke 5:1) and the Sea of Galilee or Tiberias. (John 6:1)

CHORAZIN (chora'-zin) A city near the Sea of Galilee, upbraided by Jesus for its unbelief after witnessing the miracles, and hearing the word. Along with Bethsaida and Capernaum it was doomed to destruction. (Matthew 11:21; Luke 10:13)

While Elijah hid from King Ahab the ravens brought him food. I KINGS 17: 1-7

CILICIA A province in Asia Minor bounded on the south by the Mediterranean Sea and the north by the Taurus mountains, to the west by Pamphylia, and the east by Syria. The principal city was Tarsus, birthplace of Paul. (Acts 21:39; 22:3; 23:34) Jews from Cilicia, as well as others, disputed with Stephen before he was stoned to death. (Acts 6:9) Christians living here were probably taught by Paul on his visits after his conversion. (Acts 15:23; 9:30; Galatians 1:21) He also came here with Silas confirming the church. (Acts 15:41)

COLOSSAE (Colosse) A city in Asia Minor in the province of Phrygia, not far from Laodicea. It seems Paul had not visited here prior to his Epistle to the Colossians, (Colossians 2:1) but the church was started and ministered to by Epaphras. (Colossians 1:7) and later by Archippus. (Colossians 4:17; Philemon 2) Philemon and Onesimus were faithful members of the church in Colossae. (Col. 4:9; Philem. 1)

CORINTH (cor'-inth) A city in Greece, the fourth largest in the Roman Empire, situated on an isthmus, having two harbors through which much of the commerce of the world flowed. Romans, Greeks and Jews lived here. It was a city of wealth, luxury and immorality. In 146 B.C. the city was burned by the Romans and was rebuilt in about 46 B.C. It became the capital of the Roman province, Achaia. Paul came to Corinth and lived with Aquila and Priscilla, working as a tent maker and preaching in the synagogue for 1½ years. (Acts 18:1-11) Two letters of Paul's to the Corinthians are recorded in the Bible.

CRETE A large island in the Mediterranean, also known as Candia, lying southeast of Greece. It is about 160 miles long ranging from 6 to 35 miles wide. The terrain is mountainous, its highest peak being Mount Ida, 8,065 feet high. Crete was conquered by Rome in 68-66 B.C. Paul speaks of the Cretans as "liars, evil beasts and slow bellies." (Titus 1:10-12) Jews settled here and some were present on the first day of Pentecost. (Acts 2:11) A Christian church was established in Crete and Titus visited here for a short time to put things in order and to ordain elders. (Titus 1:4-5) The ship carrying Paul

Priscilla and Aquila
ACTS 18: 1-11

to Rome as a prisoner sailed along the southern shore of Crete before it was overtaken by a fierce storm. (Acts 27:7,12,13,21)

The islands of Crete and Cyprus

CYPRUS A large island in the Mediterranean Sea off the coast of Syria. It is about 150 miles long, ranging from 5 to 50 miles wide. Many Jews, including Barnabas, lived on the island. (Acts 4:36) Christians who witnessed the stoning of Stephen returned here and peached the Gospel. (Acts 11:19) Barnabas and Paul preached in Cyprus confronting Barjesus, the sorcerer, and he was blinded. (Acts 13:4-12) After Paul and Barnabas disagreed on whether Mark should accompany them on their journey, Barnabas and Mark visited here for missionary purposes. Paul sailed past twice without landing. (Acts 21:3; 27:4)

CYRENE A city founded by the Greeks on the north coast of Africa. Many Jews resided here and some were present at Jerusalem on the day of Pentecost. (Acts 2:10)

Many of the people became converts to Christianity and preached the Gospel, including a man named Lucius. (Acts 11:20; 13:1) Simon, a Cyrenian visiting Jerusalem, was compelled to carry Jesus's cross as He was led away to be crucified. (Matthew 27:32)

D

DALMATIA (dal-ma'tia)   A Roman province east of the Adriatic Sea, also referred to as Illyricum. Titus came here perhaps to try to establish a church. (II Timothy 4:10)   Paul refers to it as a boundary of the large area in which he preached the Gospel. (Romans 15:19)

DAMASCUS (da-mas'cus)   A very ancient capital city of Syria. It was one of the ten cities originally forming the Decapolis. It was an important trade junction where three main routes met, one leading southwestward to the Mediterranean and Egypt, one to Arabia, and another across the desert to Bagdad. Parts of Damascus are very fertile, watered by canals from the rivers Abana and Pharpar. (II Kings 5:12)   Abraham pursued Lot's oppressors to a town near Damascus. (Genesis 14:15)   Eliezer, Abraham's servant, was a native of this town. (Genesis 15:2)   David captured it, fortified it, and made the people his servants. (II Samuel 8:5-6; I Chronicles 18:5-6) Rezon gathered an army and made Damascus his headquarters and reigned over Syria. When Solomon was king, he was often in conflict with Syria. (I Kings 11:23-25)

On the road to Damascus Paul replied "Lord, what wilt thou have me to do?"
ACTS 9: 1-22

It also was the capital of King Benhadad. (I Kings 15:18;20:34; II Kings 8-7; II Chronicles 16:2) Damascus became an important force in resisting the Assyrians, but it was overcome and the people were carried away as captives. (Amos 1:5) The city was rebuilt and grew prosperous. (Ezekiel 27:18) In the year 64 B.C. it was taken by the Romans and became a province. On the road to Damascus while on his way to persecute the Christians residing there, Saul of Tarsus, was struck to the ground and blinded by a great light from heaven and called by the Lord in a vision. (Acts 9:3-9) While in Damascus Saul was baptized by Ananias who was sent to him by the Lord. His sight was restored and he preached Jesus Christ in the synagogues. Jews in the city plotted to kill him, but he was let down over the wall in a basket and escaped to Jerusalem. (Acts 9:10-28)

DAN, TRIBE OF   At the time of the Exodus this tribe numbered about 60,000 men over the age of twenty years. They were among the last of the tribes to receive their portion of the land. Although it was one of the smallest areas, it was very fertile and bordered the Mediterranean Sea on the west, with the city of Joppa. (Joshua 19:40-46) As a result, some of the people apparently engaged in commerce and fishing. (Judges 5:17) Being cramped for space, some of the people went to the northernmost part of Palestine and seized the area around the town of Laish and destroyed it. Later they rebuilt the city and called it Dan. (Judges 18:1-29)

DAN A town in the extreme north of Palestine. Often it was referred to as "from Dan even to Beersheba" denoting the extreme north and south points of Palestine. (Judges 20:1; I Chronicles 21:2) It was built by the children of Dan on the site of the destroyed city of Laish in a fertile valley. (Judges 18:27-29) Here Jeroboam placed one of his golden calves in an effort to keep the Israelites of the northern kingdom from going to Jerusalem to worship in the temple. (I Kings 12:27-30; II Kings 10:29; Amos 8:14) Benhadad, in league with Asa, king of Judah, besieged and destroyed the city. (I Kings 15:20; II Chronicles 16:4) It was later rebuilt. (Ezekiel 27:19)

DAVID, CITY OF A portion of Jerusalem during David's time. When David became king over Israel, he took a stronghold from the Jebusites and called it the city of David. (II Samuel 5:6-9; I Chronicles 11:4-8) Joab was the first soldier to scale the walls of the stronghold when they attacked and he was made captain of David's army. (I Chronicle 11:6) David made it his home as did Solomon, who made it a magnificent city. The ark of God was brought here by David where it stayed in a temporary place until the

King Solomon dedicates the Temple.
I KINGS 8

temple was erected. (II Samuel 6:12,16; I Kings 8:1; I Chronicles 15:1-29; II Chronicles 5:2) David was buried here, (I Kings 2:10) as was Solomon, (I Kings 11:43) Rehoboam (I Kings 14:31) and many other kings.

DEAD SEA Called in scripture the Salt Sea (Genesis 14:3; Numbers 34:12) It is a large body of water in Palestine at the southern end of the Jordan Valley, about 50 miles long with an average breadth of 9 to 10 miles. The Dead Sea is an unusual body of water, for it constitutes a deep hole in the earth's surface, land locked, but filled with extremely salty water, even saltier than the ocean. This is due to the nature of the soil in the area which contains chlorides of sodium, magnesium and calcium. The salt is carried into the sea by the Jordan and several smaller streams and remains there because there is no outlet. The water is relieved by evaporation but the salt remains. This gives great buoyancy to the water and a bather would have difficulty sinking deep enough to swim and would emerge from the water covered with salt crystals and a greasy like substance on his skin.

DEBIR (de'bir) A city in the southern part of Judah, southwest of Hebron and formerly called Kiriath-sepher. (Joshua 15:15) It was conquered by Joshua (Joshua

DECAPOLIS A district in the northeastern part of Galilee near the Sea of Galilee, containing ten cities of Greek origin. It was rebuilt by Romans in 65 B.C. After the evil spirit was expelled by Jesus, the Gadarene demoniac published it aloud in Decapolis, (Mark 5:20) and many people followed after Jesus. (Matthew 4:25) Jesus passed through here as He traveled from Tyre and Sidon to the Sea of Galilee. (Mark 7:31)

DERBE A city in Asia Minor in the province of Lycaonia. After Paul had been stoned in Lystra while on his first missionary journey, he and Barnabus departed for Derbe where they preached the Gospel. (Acts 14:6,20,21) It was at Derbe or Lystra that he met Timothy. (Acts 16:1)

DOTHAN A city on the caravan route, not far from Shechem and Samaria. When Joseph sought his brothers, he found them near Dothan, and here he was cast into a pit until released and sold to the Midianites. (Genesis 37:17-28) It was here that Elisha was miraculously saved from the Syrians when they were temporarily struck with blindness. (II Kings 6:8-23)

Joseph cast into pit by his brothers GENESIS 37: 24

E

EBAL (e'bal) A mountain, separated from Mount Gerizim by the valley of Shechem in the promised land. It is about 3000 ft. above sea level. It was upon Mount Ebal that the curses of Israel were pronounced, and on Mount Gerizim the blessings. (Deuteronomy 11:29; 27:9-13; Joshua 8:30-35)

EDEN, GARDEN OF The first home of man. God created a garden and in it placed Adam and Eve to live and care for it. Here they were tempted by Satan, and disobeyed God by eating of the forbidden fruit. For their disobedience they were banned from the garden forever. (Genesis 2:16 to 3:24) The first promise of a Savior was given in the Garden of Eden. (Genesis 3:15-16) While the exact location of the garden has not been determined, it is believed to have been between the river Euphrates and the Tigris, the river referred to as Hiddekel. (Genesis 2:10-14)

Adam and Eve in the Garden
GENESIS 2: 8-25

EDOM   The region in which the descendants of Edom, namely Esau lived.

EDREI (ed're-i)   The capital city of Bashan. (Deuteronomy 3:10; Joshua 12:4;13:31) Here the Israelites fought with the giant Og; smote him and all his people and possessed the land. (Numbers 21:33-35; Deuteronomy 1:4;3:1-10)

Joseph explains the meaning of Pharaoh's dreams.
GENESIS 41: 1-45

EGYPT   An ancient empire comprising two kingdoms, the upper and lower Egypt, which was bounded on the north by the Mediterranean Sea, on the south by obstructing cataracts and on both sides by deserts and mountains. It was a fertile country, the soil being fed by the inundation of the Nile River, and the knowledge of irrigation. This made it a haven for people from Canaan where famine often occurred. Abraham and Lot left Bethel to sojourn in Egypt during a famine. (Genesis 12:10-20) as did Jacob and his sons at a later date. (Genesis 46:6) Joseph was brought to Egypt by the Midianites where he became an overseer in Pharaoh's kingdom. (Genesis 39:1-4) Here he interpreted Pharaoh's dream. (Genesis 41:14-33) The Israelites were enslaved in Egypt for 400 years before the Exodus. Through His leader Moses, on the night of the first passover, God led the Israelites out of Egypt. They escaped through the parted waters of the Red Sea, which then engulfed the pursuing armies of Pharaoh. (Exodus ch. 1-14) Joseph and Mary brought the infant Jesus here to escape from Herod. (Matthew 2:13)

EKRON   The most northern of the five principal cities in Philistia. (Joshua 13:3;

I Samuel 6:16-17) It was assigned to Judah (Joshua 15:45-46) and afterwards to Dan. (Joshua 19:43) Judah occupied it, but later it was reoccupied by the Philistines. The ark of God was sent here by the Philistines whence it was returned to Israel. (I Samuel 5:10) Baalzebub was the god of Ekron of whom King Ahaziah sought to inquire whether he would recover from his sickness. (II Kings 1:2-16) Judgment was pronounced upon this city by the prophets. (Jeremiah 25:20; Amos 1:8; Zephaniah 2:4; Zechariah 9:5-7)

ELAH The valley in which David slew the giant Goliath with a stone and sling. (I Samuel 21:9) It was about 11 miles southwest of Jerusalem.

ELAM A region beyond the Tigris east of Babylonia originally inhabited by descendants of Shem. (Genesis 10:22) At the time of Abraham it was the seat of an important empire under King Chedorlaomer. (Genesis 14:1-11) Elamites joined with others to prevent the rebuilding of the temple after the captivity. (Ezra 4:9) They were present in Jerusalem on the first day of Pentecost. (Acts 2:9)

ELATH A site near which the Israelites camped as they journeyed through the wilderness. (Deuteronomy 2:8) It was on the northeast coast of the Red Sea in the land of Edom, near Ezeongeber, (I Kings 9:26) and doubtless became part of David's kingdom, later to revert back to the Edomites. King Azariah (Uzziah) rebuilt it and restored it to Judah. (II Kings 14:22; II Chronicles 26:2) Subsequently it was captured by the Syrians and remained in their power for a long time. (II Kings 16:6)

ELIM The second encampment of the Israelites after crossing the Red Sea, where they found twelve wells and seventy palm trees. (Exodus 15:27) From here they entered into the wilderness of Sin. (Exodus 16:1)

EMMAUS (emma'us) A village about seven miles from Jerusalem. Jesus, on the day of His resurrection, joined two disciples, one being Cleopas, on the road to Emmaus where he revealed himself to the two. (Luke 24:13-31; Mark 16:12)

ENDOR A village belonging to the tribe of Manasseh, (Joshua 17:11) about four miles south of Mount Tabor not far from Nazareth. Here lived the woman known as the witch of Endor, with whom Saul consulted regarding the war with the Philistines. (I Samuel 28:7-14)

On the road to Emmaus
LUKE 24: 13-31

ENGEDI A town situated on the west shore of the Dead Sea belonging to the tribe of Judah. (Joshua 15:62) It was situated in a wilderness between mountains and the sea. In a nearby cave David took refuge from Saul and here he spared Saul's life.

(I Samuel 24:1-22)

EPHESUS A city in the province of Lydia on the western coast of Asia Minor. Many Jews resided at Ephesus and maintained a synagogue. (Acts 18:19) Paul, on his second missionary journey came here with Priscilla and Aquila, who remained to continue the work and to instruct Apollos. (Acts 18:24-26) On his third journey, Paul labored in Ephesus at least two years and three months. He left after a riot that was caused by the craftsmen who sold silver shrines and found their profits were endangered by the preaching of the Gospel. (Acts 19:1-41) Paul left Timothy here to prevent the church from being corrupted by false doctrine. (I Timothy 1:3) Tychicus was later sent to Ephesus with the Epistle to the Ephesians. (Ephesians 1:1; 6:21-22; II Timothy 4:12) The church in Ephesus was one of the seven churches of Asia Minor mentioned in Revelations (Revelations 1:11)

The elders of Ephesus accompany Paul to his ship.
ACTS 20: 17-38

EPHRAIM The land given to this tribe was an area in the center of Palestine extending from the Mediterranean Sea to the Jordan River, just north of the tribes of Benjamin and Dan. (Joshua 16:1-8) During the first census in the wilderness, the tribe of Ephraim had 40,000 adult males. (Numbers 1:32-33) Joshua was a member of this tribe. (Joshua 19:49-50)

ETHIOPIA (ethi-o'pia) A country south of Egypt in eastern Africa. It was called Cush in the Hebrew language. The inhabitants were tall men whose skin was colored. (Isaiah 45:14; Jeremiah 13:23) They engaged in the selling of the merchandise of their country to foreign markets. (Isaiah 45:14) Asa defeated the

"Understandest thou what thou readest?" ACTS 8: 26-39

23

Ethiopians led by Zerah at Mareshah. (II Chronicles 14:9-13; 16:8) The calling of the Ethiopians to the service of God was foretold in the Bible. (Psalms 68:31; Isaiah 45:14; Zephaniah 3:9-10) This was fulfilled in the conversion of the Ethiopian eunuch by Philip on the way to Gaza (Acts 8:26-40)

EUPHRATES (e-uphra'tes) A river rising in the mountains of Armenia, flowing through Assyria and Babylonia, through the city of Babylon. It united with the Tigris and emptied into the Persian Gulf. It was named as one of the rivers in the garden of Eden, (Genesis 2:14) and referred to by the Hebrews as "the river" (Genesis 31:21) also "the flood." (Joshua 24:2) During David and Solomon's time it constituted the northeast boundary of their vast domain. (I Kings 4:21; I Chronicles 18:3) It is referred to in the book of Revelation when angels were described as bound in the river Euphrates, (Revelation 9:14) and the sixth vial was poured out upon it. (Revelation 16:12)

EZIONGEBER (ezi-on-ge'ber) (also Eziongaber) A town by which the Israelites camped as they journeyed through the wilderness. It was on the northeast end of the Red Sea near Elath. (Deuteronomy 2:8) Solomon established a navy here from whence ships sailed to Arabia to bring back gold. (I Kings 9:26; 22:48)

F

FAIR HA'VENS A harbor in Crete near the city of Lasea, which Paul's ship entered as he was a prisoner sailing to Rome. (Acts 27:8)

G

GAD In response to its request to Moses, this tribe, along with that of Reuben, was promised an area east of the Jordan River, providing they would cross the Jordan to help drive the inhabitants out of Canaan. (Numbers 32:21-32) Their area was situated between the river Jabbok on the north and the lands given to Reuben on the south. It was especially suitable for grazing. (Joshua 13: 24-28) The tribe numbered about 45,000 males over 20 years old. (Numbers 1:24-25)

GALATIA (ga-la'tia) A Roman province in central Asia Minor

The Province of Galatia

surrounded by Bithynia, Pontus, Cappadocia, Pamphylia, Lycia and Phrygia. Most scholars feel that Paul established the churches of Galatia during his second missionary journey. As a result they date his letter to the Galatians at about 55 or 56 A.D. (Acts 16:6, 18:23; Corinthians 16:1; I Peter 1:1) (Letter to the Galatians)

GALILEE Palestine was divided into three prov‑ inces, Judea, Samaria and Galilee, all under Roman rule. Galilee comprised the northern por‑ tion extending 25 miles east and west from the Mediterranean to the Jordan River and about 60 miles north and south from the mountains of Carmel and Gilboa, to the vicinity of Mount Hermon. It originally belonged to the tribe of Naphtali, Kedesh being one of its cities. (II Kings 15:29; Joshua 20:7; 21:32)   Solomon offered twenty towns in Galilee to Hiram in payment for fir and cedar tree with which to build the temple, but he refused them. (I Kings 9:11‑13) Joseph and Mary lived in Galilee.   (Luke 1:26; 2:4)

Jesus raises Jarius' daughter
MARK 5: 35‑43

Jesus was brought up in this province and it was the scene of a large part of His ministry, the Galilean ministry, including the cities of Nazareth, Bethsaida, Capernaum, Cana, Nain and Chorazin. Twenty‑five of His thirty miracles were performed in Galilee and nineteen of His parables spoken here. It was here that He preached the Sermon on the Mount and where the transfiguration took place. Most of the apostles of Jesus came from Galilee. (Matthew 4:12 to 19:1; Mark 1:14 to 10:1; Luke 4:14 to 9:51)

GALILEE, SEA OF   A fresh water lake fed by the Jordan River in the northeastern part of Palestine. Sometimes it was also called Tiberias, (John 6:1) Gennesaret, (Luke 5:1) and Chin‑ nereth. (Numbers 34:11) . It was a deep lake with an abundance of fish, lying 680 ft. below sea level. On its borders were nine cities and also a main highway with rich traffic to Damas‑ cus. Simon, Andrew, James and John were fishing in the Sea of Galilee when Jesus called them to follow Him. (Mark 1:16‑20; Matthew 4:18‑21) Levi (Matthew) was taking in cus‑ toms beside the sea when Jesus called him. (Mark 2:13‑14) It was here also that Jesus performed the miracle of the draught of fishes. (Luke 5:1‑11) Jesus walked on the water and stilled the tempest on the Sea of Galilee. (Matthew 14:24‑34; Mark 6:45‑52)

"From henceforth thou shalt catch men."
LUKE 5: 1‑11

GATH One of the five principal cities of the Philistines. (I Samuel 6:17; 7:14; 17:52) Goliath came from Gath. (I Samuel 17:4) David captured the town, and later it was fortified by Rehoboam. (II Chronicle 11:8) It then reverted back to the Philistines only to be captured by the Syrian king Hazael. (II Kings 12:17) King Uzziah broke down the walls, (II Chronicles 26:6) and henceforth it dropped out of history.

GAZA The southernmost city of the Philistines and one of the most ancient cities in the world, (Genesis 10:19) sometimes called Azzah. (Deuteronomy 2:23; I Kings 4:24; Jeremiah 25:20) It was assigned to Judah, (Joshua 15:47) but reverted back to the Philistines. Samson carried off the gates of the city, (Judges 16:1-3) and later while in prison and blinded he ground grain here. (Judges 16:21) The last act of his life was to break down the middle pillars of the temple of Dagon where he died and many Philistines with him. (Judges 16:29-30) It was the southern boundary of Solomon's kingdom. (I Kings 4:24) Hezekiah pursued the Philistines to the gates of Gaza. (II Kings 18:8) Judgment was pronounced upon it by the prophets. (Jeremiah 25:20) Philip met the Ethiopian eunuch on the way to Gaza. (Acts 8:26)

God gave Samson strength to destroy the Philistines.
JUDGES 16: 21-31

GENNESARET (gen-nes'aret) **1.** A region of Galilee on the west shore of the Sea of Galilee. Many people were healed by Jesus in this area. (Matthew 14:34; Mark 6:53) **2.** A lake — see Galilee, Sea of.

GERIZIM A high mountain in the promised land, separated from Mount Ebal by the valley of Shechem. It was 2,800 ft. above sea level. Upon this mountain the blessings of Israel were pronounced and on Mount Ebal the curses. (Deuteronomy 11:29; 27:9-13; Joshua 8:30-35) Jotham spoke his parable to the men of Shechem from the top of this mountain. (Judges 9:7-21) This is assumed to be the mountain referred to by the woman of Samaria as she spoke to Jesus at the well. (John 4:20-21)

GESHUR (ge'shur) A district in Syria east of the Jordan River. It was allotted to Manasseh but not overthrown by them. (Joshua 13:13) David married the daughter of the ruler of this principality. (II Samuel 3:3) Absalom fled to Geshur after killing

Amnon, (II Samuel 13:37-38) and Joab returned him from thence to Jerusalem (II Samuel 14:23)

GETHSEMANE (geth-sem'a-ne) A garden near the Mount of Olives east of Jerusalem beyond the brook Kidron. Here Jesus often went to pray and it was the scene of His agony and betrayal. (Matthew 26:36-56; Mark 14:32-52; Luke 22:39-53; John 18:1-12)

Christ praying
MATTHEW 26: 36

GIBEAH (gib'e-ah) A village belonging to the tribe of Benjamin, (Judges 19:14) also called Gibeah of Saul. (I Samuel 11:4) It was the scene of an inhuman crime committed by the inhabitants against the concubine of a Levite, (Judges 19:1-30) for which the Benjaminites were nearly destroyed by the Israelites. (Judges 20:1-48) It was also the birthplace of Saul and his residence after he became king, (I Samuel 10:26; 11:4; 15:34) and where seven of his offspring were hanged by the Gibeonites. (II Samuel 21:6-9)

GIBEON (gib'e-on) A city inhabited by Hivites at the time of Joshua. (Joshua 11:19) To avoid the fate of Ai and Jericho, the Hivites made a treaty with Joshua under false pretenses. When discovered, Joshua made them slaves to the Israelites. (Joshua 9:1-27) Gibeon was allotted to Benjamin and made a Levitical city. (Joshua 18:25; 21:17) Solomon went to Gibeon to worship because there was an altar of the Lord. It was here that the Lord appeared to him in a dream and in response to his request, God granted him great wisdom and understanding. (I Kings 3: 4:15)

GIHON 1. One of the four rivers in the Garden of Eden (Genesis 2:13)
2. A spring outside Jerusalem from which the city received its water supply. (II Chronicles 32:30) Here Solomon was anointed as king of Israel. (I Kings 1:32-40)

GILBOA (gil-bo'a) A mountain in Israel on which Saul was defeated by the Philistines and where he and his three sons met their death. (I Samuel 31:1-6; I Chronicles 10:1-8)

GILEAD A large mountainous region east of the Jordan River, reaching from the upper end of the Dead Sea to the Sea of Galilee. The scenery is beautiful and the hills are fertile and covered with forests. A covenant between Jacob and Laban took place on Mount Gilead and Jacob called the place Mizpah of Galead. (Genesis 31:20-49) The southern half was assigned to the tribe of Gad and the northern half to the half tribe of Manasseh. (Deuteronomy 3:12,13; Joshua 13:24-31)

Jacob and Laban make a covenant
GENESIS 31: 44-49

GILGAL (gil'gal) 1. The first encampment of the Israelites in Canaan after crossing the Jordan. God had dried up the river to allow them to pass and they placed twelve stones as a memorial. (Joshua 4:19-24) It was one of the cities from which Samuel judged the people. (I Samuel 7:16) Here Saul preparing for battle with the Philistines offered a burnt offering himself rather than waiting for Samuel and for this was rejected by God. (I Samuel 13:4-14) Later when he failed to destroy Agag he was again rejected and God's spirit withdrew from him. (I Samuel 15:20-21, 16:14) 2. A village from whence Elijah and Elisha came to Bethel and where Elisha performed a miracle. (II Kings 2:1; 4:38-44)

GOLGOTHA (gol'go-tha) See Calvary

GOMORRAH (go-mor'rah) A city near Sodom on the plain of Jordan which God destroyed with fire and brimstone because of the wickedness of the people. (Genesis 19:24-25)

GOSHEN The northeastern section of Egypt where Pharaoh allowed the Hebrews to live and care for their flocks when Jacob and his sons came to Egypt. (Genesis 47:27) Referred to in Exodus as Rameses. (Exodus 12:37)

GREECE A small but highly cultured country in southeastern Europe, bordered on the south by the Mediterranean Sea and on the east by the Aegean Sea. It was conquered by the Romans but the Greek language, culture and philosophy continued to influence the civilized world and at the time of Christ the Greek language was almost universally spoken. Paul brought Christianity to Greece on his visits to Philippi, Athens, Thessalonica, Berea, and Corinth. (Acts ch. 17 & 18)

H

HAMATH (ha'math) An early settlement of the Canaanites. (Genesis 10:18) Later it was a city in northern Assyria ruled by Toi in David's time. (II Samuel 8:9) Solomon took it and made it a store city. (II Chronicles 8:3-4) It belonged to Judah after the kingdom was divided, but Jeroboam II captured it along with Damascus and kept it for the northern kingdom, (II Kings 14:28) until it fell into the hands of the Assyrians. (II Kings 17:24)

HARAN (ha'ran) A city in Mesopotamia where Terah, Abraham and Lot dwelt after leaving Ur of the Chaldees. (Genesis 11:31) It was here that God first told Abraham He would make of him a great nation. (Genesis 12:1-5) Terah died here. (Genesis 11:32)

Abraham's seed was to be numbered as the stars. GENESIS 15: 5

28

HAROD A well near Mount Gilboa where Gideon was instructed by God to choose those who would fight against the Midianites by the manner in which they drank water from the well. Three hundred men were chosen. (Judges 7:1-8)

The Midianites fled as Gideon and his men blew their trumpets.   JUDGES 7: 16-23

HAZEROTH (haz'eroth) A camping place of the children of Israel in the wilderness beyond Kibroth-hattaavah (Numbers 11:35) It was here that Aaron and Miriam murmured against Moses because he married an Ethiopian woman and Miriam became leprous. She was shut out of camp for seven days. (Numbers 12)

HAZOR A principal Canaanite city in northern Palestine. Its king, Jabin, summoned help from neighboring kings to fight against Joshua and the Israelites, but Joshua captured the city and burned it and destroyed the people. (Joshua 11:1-14) It was rebuilt and assigned to the tribe of Naphtali. (Joshua 19:36) When Deborah was a judge over Israel, the city was ruled by another King Jabin, who was defeated and slain by the Israelites. (Judges 4:1-24; I Samuel 12:9) The inhabitants were carried away as captives by King Tiglath-pileser. (II Kings 15:29)

HEBRON An ancient city in the hill country of Judah also called Kirjatharba. (Joshua 15:54) The city existed as early as the time of Abraham. Sarah died here and Abraham bought the cave of Machpelah near Hebron in which to bury her. (Genesis 23:2-20) Isaac and Jacob sojourned here for awhile. (Genesis 35:27; 37:14) It was visited by the spies who were sent by Moses to spy on Canaan. (Numbers 13:22) The inhabitants allied themselves with King Adoni-zedek and were defeated and slain by Joshua. (Joshua 10:1-27, 36,39) The Canaanites re-established the city and later it was claimed by Judah as their allotted territory but Caleb retook it as his possession. (Judges 1:10-15) David sent part of the spoils of Ziklag to Hebron. (I Samuel 30:31) Later he ruled here as king of Judah for 7½ years. (II Samuel 2:1-3, 11, 32; 5:1-5,13; I Kings 2:11; Chronicles 11:1-3; 12-23-38; I Chronicles 29:27) Several of his sons were born in Hebron. (II Samuel 3:2-5; I Chronicle 3:1-4) Abner was buried here, (II Samuel 3:32) and with him the head of Ishbosheth, son of Saul. (II Samuel 4:12)

HERMON A snow capped mountain on the eastern border of Palestine rising over

9,000 ft. above sea level. It was the northern limit of the conquests of Joshua (Deuteronomy 3:8-9) (Joshua 11:3, 17; 12:1; 13:5, 11) It is believed that the transfiguration of Jesus took place on Mount Hermon.

HESHBON The city of the Amorite king, Sihon, taken originally from the Moabites but conquered by the Israelites under Moses. (Numbers 21:25-30) It was assigned to the Reubenites who rebuilt it, (Numbers 32:37; Joshua 13:17) and later it became the possession of Gad, (Joshua 13:26) and a Levitical city. (Joshua 21:39; I Chronicles 6:81) Apparently it was held by the Moabites again in Isaiah and Jeremiah's time. (Isaiah 15:4; 16:8-9; Jeremiah 48:2,33,34)

The Transfiguration of Jesus   MATTHEW 17: 1-9

HIDDEKEL (hid'de-kel) The ancient name for the Tigris River, mentioned as one of the rivers flowing out of Eden. (Genesis 2:10-14) Its source is in the mountains of Armenia and it enters into the Euphrates as it flows down to the Persian Gulf. It is a place where Daniel saw a vision. (Daniel 10:4 etc.)

HINNOM, VALLEY OF (hin'-nom) A deep narrow ravine southwest of Jerusalem. It was the boundary between Judah and Benjamin. (Joshua 15:8; 18:16) On its eastern extremity Solomon had altars erected for his heathen wives. (I Kings 11:7) During the reign of Ahaz and Manasseh, the horrible rite of sacrificing children by forcing them to walk through fire was practiced. (II Chronicles 28:1-3; 33:6) King Josiah broke down the altars and made the area ceremonially unclean by polluting it with human bones. (II Kings 23:10-14)

HOR A mountain on the boundary line of Edom (Numbers 33:37) upon which Aaron died. (Numbers 20:25-29)

HOREB The mount of God, also referred to as Sinai. Opinions are that Sinai was the peak or summit. Here Moses encountered the burning bush (Exodus 3:1-6) and also smote the rock for water to drink. (Exodus 17:6) At Horeb the Lord appeared to the Israelites as a cloudy pillar (Exodus 33:4-11) and Moses put the two tablets of stone in the ark. (I Kings 8:9; II Chronicles 5:10)

Moses and the burning bush
EXODUS 3: 1-6

I

ICONIUM (i·co'ni·um) A city in Lycaonia in Asia Minor visited by Paul and Barnabas on the first missionary journey. The unbelieving Jews of this city stirred up trouble and took part in the stoning of Paul. (Acts 13:51; 14:1-5,19,21; 16:2)

INDIA An area on the lower Indus River, which was taken by Darius the Great. India formed the eastern boundary of the Persian Empire as referred to in the book of Esther. (Esther 1:1, 8-9) Some of the products of India were no doubt brought to the land of Israel by camel caravans which passed through.

ISRAEL, KINGDOM OF After the death of Solomon, his son Rehoboam became king. He was relentless in his demands upon the people and when under Jeroboam's leadership they asked for a less oppressive government, Rehoboam refused. Ten tribes rebelled and formed the Kingdom of Israel, or the Northern Kingdom. The tribes making up the Kingdom of Israel were Reuben, Gad, half Manasseh, Ephraim, Issachar, Zebulun, Naphtali, Asher, Dan and part of Benjamin. Jeroboam became their king. The tribe of Judah and part of Benjamin united to form the kingdom of Judah with Rehoboam as their king. The territory of Israel reached from Bethel on the south to Dan on the north as religious centers. Shechem was built as the first capital, but later the capital was moved to Tirzah (I Kings ch. 12; 15:21) The Kingdom of Israel lasted a little over 200 years and was destroyed by Assyria in 721 B.C.

ISRAEL, LAND OF Israel was a name given to Jacob after his struggle with an angel of God at the river Jabbok. (Genesis 32:22-30) His descendants were called Israelites and the area that was given to the twelve tribes in Canaan was referred to as the land of Israel until the time of the divided kingdom.

The Land of Israel
The Twelve Tribes

ISSACHAR (is'sa-char)   The territory allotted to this tribe was above the lands given to Manasseh. Mount Tabor was on its northern border. A large part of its area was a low fertile plain. Issachar was one of the larger tribes with males over twenty years old numbering 54,000 during the first census. (Numbers 1:28-29)

ITALY   This geographical area frequently referred to in Acts was relatively the same as we today know Italy. Rome was its capital and the greater part of the then civilized world was ruled from here. Aquila and Priscilla, both of Jewish descent, lived here for a time. (Acts 18:2)   It was Paul's intent to visit Rome as stated in his letter to the Christians in Rome, (Romans 1:10-12) after he had completed his work where he was then engaged. His return to Jerusalem, however, changed all of his plans. When Paul made his appeal to Caesar to come to Rome for a hearing, his ship sailed along the coast of Italy. (Acts 27:1; 28:13-16)   The Christians of Italy are mentioned in the closing verses of the letters to the Hebrews. (Hebrews 13:24)

J

JABBOK (jab'bok)   A brook east of the Jordan River, flowing into that river about midway between the Sea of Galilee and the Dead Sea. Jacob, returning to Canaan, forded the brook and on the southern boundary wrestled with an angel of the Lord, and his name was changed from Jacob to Israel. (Genesis 32:22-32)   Near here he reconciled with Esau. (Genesis 33:1-15)   It was the western boundary of the land of the Ammonites, separating it from the Amorites. (Numbers 21:24; Deuteronomy 2:37; 3:16; Joshua 12:2)

JABESH-GILEAD (ja-besh-gil'ead)   A town of Gilead. The inhabitants here were destroyed by the children of Israel for failing to war against the Benjaminites for their crime against the Levi's concubine. Only 400 virgins were spared. (Judges 21:8-14)   It was reoccupied. During the reign of Saul, the city was besieged by the Ammonites. The Ammonite king, Nabash, made a condition that he would not take the city if every man had his right eye thrust out. King Saul came to their rescue, drove out the Ammonites and preserved the people. (I Samuel 11:1-11)   In gratitude, when Saul's body and those of his sons were fastened to the walls of Bethshean, the men of Jabesh-gilead carried the corpses to their city, burned them and buried the ashes, (I Samuel 31:11-13; I Chronicles 10:11-12) from where they were later removed to the sepulcher of Kish. (II Samuel 2:4-7; 21:12-14)

JACOB'S WELL   A well located in Sychar, a city of Samaria. Jacob used the well, and also his sons and his cattle. (John 4:5,6,12)   The water was good but difficult to reach, as the well was deep.

Jesus and the Samaritan woman
JOHN 4: 4-26

It is thought to have been 75 ft. deep. (John 4:11) Jesus met a woman of Samaria at the well and after asking for a drink, He revealed Himself to her as the Christ. (John 4:4-26)

JEHOVAH-JIREH (je-ho-vah-ji'reh) The name given by Abraham to the place where he was prepared to sacrifice his son, Isaac, as God had directed to test his faith. When God's angel stopped him he found a ram caught in a thicket which he sacrificed instead. (Genesis 22:1-14)

JEHOVAH-NISSI (je-ho-vah-nis'si) The name given by Moses to an altar built by him at Rephidim in the wilderness as a memorial of Israel's victory over the Amalekites. Moses, with the rod of God, held up his hands and the Israelites prevailed, but when his arms were weary and came down, the Amalekites prevailed. Aaron and Hur held up Moses' hands until the enemy was defeated. (Exodus 17:8-16)

God tests Abraham's faith when He asks him to sacrifice Isaac.
GENESIS 22: 1-14

JERICHO An ancient walled city situated in the valley of the Jordan River. It was west of the river, just north of the Dead Sea. It must have been an important city for it is mentioned often in Scriptures. The two spies sent out by Joshua from Shittim lodged with Rahab in Jericho. (Joshua 2:1-24) After which Joshua led the Israelites over the Jordan into Canaan, pitching camp near the city. By the command of God, the armed men of the Israelites destroyed Jericho. They went around the city once a day for six days with the Ark of the Covenant and seven priests blowing on trumpets. On the seventh day they compassed the city seven times and when a signal was given by a loud blast of the trumpets, the men shouted and the walls of the city fell. The Israelites went in, slew all the people but Rahab and her family. They destroyed everything except silver, gold and other valuables that were taken for the treasury of the Lord. (Joshua 6) Achan coveted and took silver, and gold from Jericho for himself, transgressing God's command, for which he was put to death. (Joshua 7:18-26) It was assigned to the tribe of Benjamin. (Joshua 18:21) Jericho was not mentioned again for some time, but apparently was rebuilt and established as a prominent place. David's servants were embarrassed because Hanun had shaven off their beards and cut their garments in the middle. They went to Jericho until their beards grew. (II Samuel 10:4-5) During Elijah's time there was a community of the prophets here. It was at Jericho that Elijah went up to heaven in a whirlwind. (II Kings 2:1-5) As Jesus was leaving Jericho, He restored sight to blind Bartimaeus. (Matthew 20:29-34; Mark 10: 46-52; Luke 18:35-43) Jesus abode here

The walls of Jericho fell down flat.
JOSHUA 6: 1-21

with Zacchaeus the publican and brought salvation to him and his household. (Luke 19: 1-10) Jericho is also mentioned in the parable of the Good Samaritan. (Luke 10:30-37)

JERUSALEM   The Holy City and capital of Palestine. It is situated on a rocky plateau comprised of three hills, and surrounded by ravines. The city is centrally located east of the Mediterranean Sea and west of the Dead Sea, about parallel to the northern end of the Dead Sea. The Jebusites inhabited Jerusalem when the Israelites came to Canaan. Its king was slain by Joshua (Joshua 10:23-26) and the city was taken by the men of Judah. (Judges 1:8) It was assigned to Benjamin. (Joshua 18:28) Jerusalem came into prominence in connection with Biblical history in the time of David. During this time it was sometimes referred to as Salem or city of David. David made it his capital (II Samuel 5:6-7) as well as the religious center of the kingdom. He built the walls of Jerusalem for defense purposes (II Samuel 5:9) and these walls were later expanded by Solomon to include a larger area. David also brought the Ark of the Covenant to Jerusalem, (II Samuel 6:12) and began plans for the temple, the building of which was carried out by Solomon. (I Kings 5:3-5) The city prospered under Solomon. In addition to the temple, he built the royal palace, (I Kings 9:10) and made many other improvements. During the divided kingdom,

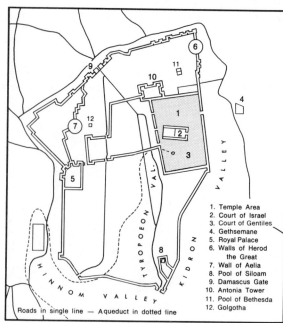

1. Temple Area
2. Court of Israel
3. Court of Gentiles
4. Gethsemane
5. Royal Palace
6. Walls of Herod the Great
7. Wall of Aelia
8. Pool of Siloam
9. Damascus Gate
10. Antonia Tower
11. Pool of Bethesda
12. Golgotha

Roads in single line — Aqueduct in dotted line

Jerusalem became the capital of the kingdom of Judah. (I Kings 14:21) It was besieged and completely destroyed by Nebuchadnezzar, (II Kings 24:10; 25:1) and the inhabitants of Judah were carried into exile by the Babylonians. (II Kings 24:15) The city lay in ruins until its walls were rebuilt by Nehemiah about 445 B.C., (Nehemiah 2:17) and the temple rebuilt by Zerubbabel. (Ezra 5:2) In subsequent years the city was invaded by various powers who desecrated the temple. The Maccabees retook it and purified the temple, (See Maccabees) but it was again dispoiled. In the year 37 B.C. Herod the

Nehemiah directs the rebuilding of the walls of Jerusalem.   NEHEMIAH 2: 17-4: 23

great repaired the walls of the city and built the temple which existed at the time of Christ. In 70 A.D. the Romans under Titus laid siege to and completely destroyed Jerusalem as foretold by Jesus. (Luke 19:41-44; 21:20-24) The infant Jesus was brought to Jerusalem and presented to the Lord. At this time Simeon took Him in his arms and spoke the words of the Nunc Dimittis. He later returned as a boy of twelve and on various other occasions. (Luke 2:22-38, 2:40-50; John 2:13-25, 7:14-53) He made His final entry into the city when He triumphantly rode into Jerusalem on a donkey while the people strewed palms along His path. (Matthew 21:1-17; Mark 11:1-11; Luke 19:28-40) It was in an upper room in Jerusalem that Jesus instituted the Last Supper. (Matthew 26:17-30; Mark 14:12-26; Luke 22:1-20) Jesus' trial prior to His

The Last Supper   MATTHEW 26: 17-30

crucifixion on Golgotha outside of Jerusalem, took place here. (Matthew 26:57 to 27:50; Mark 14:43 to 15:42; Luke 22:47 to 23:49; John 18:1 to 19:37) After His resurrection, Jesus appeared to His disciples in the city. (Mark 16:14; Luke 24:36-48; John 20:19-23) The disciples were gathered together in Jerusalem on the first day of Pentecost. (Acts Ch. 2) Paul journeyed to Jerusalem where he conferred with the disciples, visited the temple and preached the Gospel. (Acts 21:15-40)

JEZREEL (jez'reel) A fortified walled town situated on a plain near Mount Gilboa. (I Kings 21:23; II Kings 9:17) It was in the territory of Issachar. (Joshua 19:17-18) The Israelites encamped at a fountain in Jezreel just before the battle of Gilboa in which Saul and his sons died. (I Samuel 29:1; II Samuel 4:4) Ishbosheth, Saul's son, reigned over this city for two years until he was murdered. (II Samuel 2:8-9) Ahab had a palace here. (I Kings 18:45-46) Naboth was a native of Jezreel and had a vineyard adjacent to Ahab's palace, which Ahab coveted. Through Jezebel's scheming, Naboth was stoned to death and Ahab took possession of the vineyards. (I Kings 21:1-29) Jezebel met her death when she was thrown from a window of the palace by two servants at the command of Jehu. (II Kings 9:10,30-37) The heads of Ahab's 70 sons were piled at the gates of Jezreel by order of Jehu. (II Kings 10:1-11) That the blood of Jezreel should be avenged was prophesied by Hosea (Hosea 1:4)

JOPPA (jop'pa) An ancient city on the Mediterranean Sea. It was a harbor to which Hiram floated fir trees of Mount Lebanon from Tyre. From here they were carried to Jerusalem for use in building the temple. (II Chronicles 2:16) After the captivity, trees were again brought down in the same manner for the rebuilding of the temple under Ezra. (Ezra 3:7) Jonah embarked at Joppa when he went to Tarshish and on the way was swallowed up by a great fish. (Jonah 1:3) Peter miraculously raised Tabitha, also known as Dorcas, from the dead in Joppa. (Acts 9:36-41) As a result, he received many followers for Christ. (Acts 9:42) He spent some time residing with Simon, the tanner, and here he saw the vision of the great sheet let down from heaven, (Acts 9:43) after which he was summoned by Cornelius to come to Caesarea. (Acts 10:17-23)

Dorcas was full of good works and almsdeeds.   ACTS 9: 36

JORDAN The principal river in Palestine, which rises from three major sources, and winds down its course for 200 miles. It descends, as its name implies, from its source which is 1,000 ft. above sea level to the Sea of Galilee which is 682 ft. below sea level, winding down a tortuous path to the Dead Sea, 1,292 ft. below sea level. The banks of the river south of the Sea of Galilee are fringed with trees and shrubs, but as it drops down to a lower level towards the Dead Sea, it flows through a tropical area. Few towns have been built along

Naaman washes himself in the river Jordan and is healed.
II KINGS 5: 8-14

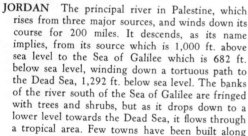

the river, due to the intense heat. In ancient times, it was infested with wild animals and subject to invasion by the Arabs. At certain times, the Jordan overflowed its banks and the plains became very fertile. When Abraham and Lot separated, Lot chose the plain of Jordan. (Genesis 13:10) It was referred to in the Bible as a boundary and frontier, (Genesis 32:10; Numbers 34:10-12; Deuteronomy 3:20; 27:4; Joshua 1:2; 13-23) and a military frontier. (Judges 7:24; 12:5) Before entering the promised land, Joshua and the Israelites came to

The Baptism of Jesus MATTHEW 3: 13-17

the Jordan, (Joshua 3:1) and God held back the waters to allow them to pass over into Canaan. (Joshua 3:13-17) Elijah parted the waters of Jordan so that he and Elisha could pass over. (II Kings 2:7-8) Elisha did likewise on his return. (II Kings 2:13-14) Naaman, a Syrian general, was cleansed of leprosy by washing seven times in the Jordan as directed by Elisha. (II Kings 5:10-14) John, the Baptist baptized in the Jordan, (Mark 1:4-5; Luke 3:2-14) and it was here that Jesus was baptized. (Matthew 3:13-17)

JUDAH, KINGDOM OF After the ten tribes rebelled against the tyranny of Rehoboam and formed the kingdom of Israel, the tribe of Judah and part of Benjamin remained as the kingdom of Judah. Their territory was in the southern part of Palestine with Jerusalem as their capital. (I Kings Ch. 12) There was long and continued war between Israel and Judah after the division of the kingdom. Judah lasted a little over 300 years and was destroyed by Babylonia in 587 B.C.

JUDAH, TRIBE OF This was the largest of the tribes with almost 75,000 adult males when Moses numbered the people in the wilderness of Sinai. (Numbers 1:26-27) The tribe of Judah was the first to take possession of its land after crossing the Jordan River. It occupied a greater part of southern Palestine stretching from the Mediterranean Sea to the Dead Sea, and extending over 50 miles from north to south. (Joshua 15:1-12) Although quite hilly and rocky, the land was well adapted to the growing of grapes and for pasturage.

JUDEA The southernmost province of Palestine. It was the kingdom of Herod the Great, and after his death became the kingdom of Archelaus. After his banishment it was placed under Roman administration and governed through procurators. Pontius Pilate was governor when Jesus carried out His ministry. (Luke 3:1) Judea was bounded on the north by Samaria, and on the south by the desert. The eastern boundary included the wilderness of Judea, a vast desert area extending from the Dead Sea and west to the hill country. In this wilder-

John preaches repentance.
MATTHEW 3: 1-12

ness John the Baptist prepared for his mission and preached repentance. (Matthew 3:1-3; Luke 3:2) Here Jesus was tempted by Satan. (Luke 4:1)

K

KADESH also **Kadesh-barnea** A place where the Israelites twice encamped enroute to Canaan from Egypt. It was just south of Palestine in the wilderness of Paran, (Numbers 13:26) and in the wilderness of Zin. (Numbers 20:1; 33:36) Water seemed to be the reason the Israelites stayed in this area for an extended time, for there was a supply after Moses struck a rock twice with a rod making water come out abundantly. Because he struck the rock instead of speaking to it as God told him, was one of the reasons why Moses and Aaron were not allowed to enter the promised land. (Numbers 20:7-12) Miriam died and was buried in Kadesh. (Numbers 20:1) From here Moses sent messengers to Edom requesting permission to pass through their country to get to Canaan, but they refused. (Numbers 20:14-21)

Moses striking rock for water
NUMBERS 20: 7-12

Moses sent out spies from Kadesh to explore Canaan. (Numbers 13:1-33) They returned with their report, and when the people rebelled and threatened to choose a leader to help them return to Egypt, God sentenced them to 40 years of wandering in the wilderness. (Numbers 14:1-39; Deuteronomy 2:14) For 40 years the children of Israel lived a nomad life wandering about, but not advancing towards their goal. They assembled together frequently at Kadesh. (Deuteronomy 1:2; 1:46; 2:14; Numbers 33:36)

KEDESH 1. A town near the southern border of Judah, (Joshua 15:23) thought to be different from Kadash-barnea. (Joshua 15:3)
2. A fenced city allotted to Naphtali (Joshua 19:37) and a city of refuge. (Joshua 20:7-9) It was called Kedesh Naphtali to distinguish it from other towns with the same name. (Judges 4:6) Its king was slain by Joshua. (Joshua 12:22) Under the judges, Deborah went with Barak to Kedesh to help him defeat Sisera at Mount Tabor. (Judges 4:6-17) Later its inhabitants were carried off as captives to Assyria by Tiglath-pileser. (II Kings 15:29)
3. A city in the tribe of Issachar, also a Levitical city. (I Chronicles 6:72) Also known as Kishion. (Joshua 19:20; 21:28)

KERIOTH A town in Judah near the southern border, (Joshua 15:25) thought to be the birthplace of Judas Iscariot, as his name alludes to Kerioth.

KIBROTH-HATTAAVAH A camping place of the children of Israel, in the wilderness between Mount Sinai and Hazeroth. (Numbers 33:16-17; Deuteronomy 9:22) The people gathered quail all day, all night and the following day, then hoarded them for which God caused a plague to descend upon them and many died and were buried at Kibroth-hattaavah. (Numbers 11:31-35)

KIDRON (also Cedron) A valley to the east of Jerusalem. It begins north of the city and continues south and east, dropping below sea level as it takes its course through the wilderness of Judea to the Dead Sea. It has a dry bed, except in winter when it is fed by heavy rains and the brook Kidron flows through it. The Kidron separated Jerusalem from the Mount of Olives and had to be crossed by anyone going to Bethany or Jericho. David crossed the brook as he fled from Absalom. (II Samuel 15:23) Asa, Josiah and Hezekiah used the valley as a dumping place for idols. (I Kings 15:13; II Kings 23:4-20; II Chronicles 29:16; 30:14) It was also the common burying ground for Jerusalem. (II Kings 23:6) Jesus crossed the brook Kidron when He went into Gethsemane to pray before He was betrayed by Judas Iscariot. (John 18:1)

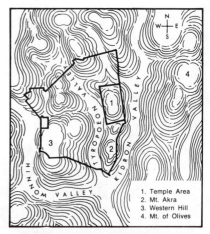

1. Temple Area
2. Mt. Akra
3. Western Hill
4. Mt. of Olives

Topographic map of the Kidron Valley
City of Jerusalem (enclosed area)

KIRIATH-JEARIM (kir-i-ath-je'a-rim) A Canaanite town originally belonging to the Gibeonites. (Joshua 9:17) It was on the western boundary line between the tribes of Judah and Benjamin, (Joshua 15:9; 18:14-15) but pertained to Judah. (Joshua 15:60; Judges 18:12) The exact location is not known, but it is believed to have been in the hill country not far from Jerusalem. After the Ark of the Covenant was returned by the Philistines, it rested in Kiriath-jearim for 20 years until David brought it up to Jerusalem. (I Samuel 6:21; 7:1-2) Some

The Ark of the Covenant 1 SAMUEL 7: 1-2

of the inhabitants returned after the captivity. (Nehemiah 7:29) In Ezra 2:25 the name appears as Kirjatharim and in Joshua 15:60 as Kirjathbaal. Also referred to as Baalah. (Joshua 15:9)

KISHON A river in Palestine second only to the Jordan River in importance. It rises in the foothills of Mount Tabor and Gilboa, running in a northwesterly direction through the plain of Esdraelon, emptying into the Mediterranean Sea at the foot of Mount Carmel. Much of the year the river bed is dry, but during the winter rains it becomes deep and marshy and almost impassable. Sisera's army was swept away by the waters when they attempted to ford the river while fleeing from Barak. (Judges 5:20-21) Deborah refers to it as "that ancient river" in her song of thanksgiving.

(Judges 5:21)   After the trial on Mount Carmel between God and Baal, Elijah took the prophets of Baal down to the river Kishon and slew them.   (I Kings 18:40)

L

LACHISH (la'chish)   A fortified city in Canaan first occupied by Amorites, situated in the lowlands of Judah. Its king, Japhia, was allied with Adonizedek and three other kings to help overthrow the Gibeonites because they had made a pact with the Israelites, but Japhia was captured and hanged. (Joshua 10:3-27) Joshua seized the town, (Joshua 10:31-34; 12:11) and Rehoboam rebuilt and fortified it. (II Chronicles 11:9) King Amaziah sought refuge behind the walls of Lachish but was pursued and slain. (II Kings 14:19; II Chronicles 25:27) Sennacherib, king of Assyria, besieged the town and from a camp nearby sent a demand for the surrender of Jerusalem. (II Kings 18:13.14.17; II Chronicles 32:9; Isaiah 36:2) Lachish is charged with being the beginning of the sin to the daughter of Zion. (Micah 1:13) The city was destroyed by Nebuchadnezzar (Jeremiah 34:7) and reinhabited after the captivity. (Nehemiah 11:30)

LAODICEA (la-od-i-ce'a)   A city in Phrygia of Asia Minor. It was a rich manu-facturing center for clothing and wool, and the seat of a medical school. Epaphras preached the Gospel here. (Colossians 4:13) Paul directed the epistle to the Colossians to be read to the church in Laodicea and implies that a letter had been written to the Laodiceans, however no record has been found of this letter. (Colossians 4:16) Paul had great concern for the church here. (Colossians 2:1) Laodicea is one of the seven churches of Asia mentioned in the book of Revelation. (Revelation 1:11; 3:14)

LEBANON   A lofty snow capped mountain range in Syria, forming the northwest boundary of Palestine. (Deuteronomy 1:7;11:24; Joshua 1:4;11:17;12:7;13:5) Its streams made the valley fertile, and the mountains were covered with gigantic cedars, fir trees or cypresses. (Isaiah 60:13; Solomon 5:15) Hiram sent cedar and fir trees from Mount Lebanon to Solomon for use in building the temple and his palace. Solomon supplied man power for cutting down the trees. (I Kings 5:6-14; II Kings 19:23) When the temple was rebuilt after the captivity, lumber was again supplied from the Lebanon Mountains. (Ezra 3:7) The trees of Lebanon were also used for the building of ships and their masts. (Ezekiel 27:5)

LIBYA   A desert country west of Egypt with its northern border on the Mediterranean Sea, and the vast desert on the south. It is thought to be the country of the ancient Lubims related to the generations of Noah. (Genesis 10:13; II Chronicles 12:3; 16:8) The Roman Libya extended from Egypt across the entire African continent excluding the small Greek settlement of Cyrene and Barca as well as the Phoenician colonies of Carthage, Utica and Hippo. (Ezekiel 30:5;38:5) Its capital was the city of Cyrene.

Jews resided in Libya and were present in Jerusalem on the day of Pentecost. (Acts 2:10)

LYCAONIA (lyc·a·o'nia) A Roman province in Asia Minor bounded on the north by Galatia, on the south by Cilicia, on the east by Cappadocia and on the west by Phrygia. It was rugged country and suitable mainly for grazing. The people spoke in a manner peculiar to their area. (Acts 14:11) The three main cities of Lycaonia were Iconium, Derbe and Lystra. Paul and Barnabas visited these cities preaching the Gospel. (Acts 13:51 to 14:23) Paul revisited Derbe and Lystra where he met Timothy. (Acts 16:1)

Lycaonia and surrounding provinces

LYCIA (ly'cia) A Roman province in Asia Minor jutting out into the Mediterranean Sea. Patara and Myra were cities in the province visited by Paul. (Acts 21:1·2; 27:5·6)

LYDDA A large village southwest of Joppa probably called Lod in the Old Testament. In this city, Peter cured Aeneas who was sick of the palsy and many people became Christians. (Acts 9:32·35) From here he was summoned to come to Joppa when Tabitha, or Dorcas, had died. (Acts 9:38)

LYSTRA A city of Lycaonia. Paul fled to this city from Iconium when his life was threatened. It was here that he was stoned and left for dead. (Acts 14) He here also healed a man who had been crippled from birth. (Acts 14:8·12) It was in Lystra or Derbe that Paul first met Timothy. (Acts 16:1)

LEVITICAL CITIES Since the Levites received no inheritance in the land, (Numbers 18:20) the rest of the tribes were commanded to give them cities within their territory in which to dwell, including lands around the cities for the pasturage of their cattle. Forty·eight such cities were designated which included six cities of refuge. (Numbers 35:2·8) The Levites received the tithes from the people for their services in connection with the tabernacle. (Numbers 18:21:24)

M

MACEDONIA A country directly north of Greece. It was not mentioned in the Old Testament. In 168 B.C. it was conquered by the Romans and became a Roman province. It was Macedonia where Paul first preached the Gospel in Europe. A vision appeared to him summoning him to come here to preach. (Acts 16:9) At that time he passed through the Macedonian cities of Neapolis, Philippi, Amphipolis, Apollonia, Thessalonica and Berea. (Acts 16:9 to 17:14) After he departed he left Timothy and Silas to minister to the churches. (Acts 17:14-15, 18:5) Paul revisited it later. (Acts 20:1; II Corinthians 2:13, 7:5; I Timothy 1:3) Erastus joined Timothy in the work. (Acts 19:22) Gaius, Aristarchus, Secundus and Sopater, Paul's co-workers, were from Macedonia. (Acts 19:29 & 20:4) The converts here made a contribution to help the poor in Jerusalem, (Romans 15:26) and also administered to Paul. (II Corinthians 8:1-5) The church at Philippi was the first to perform these acts of charity. (Philippians 4:15)

MACHPELAH (mach-pe'lah) A place purchased by Abraham from Ephron for 400 shekels of silver. (Genesis 23:9-17) It was near Hebron in Canaan. The cave of Machpelah was made a burying place for Abraham's family. (Genesis 23:20) He buried his wife, Sarah in the cave, (Genesis 23:19) and his sons, Isaac and Ishmael, buried him there. (Genesis 25:9-10) Here also Isaac, Rebekah, Leah and Jacob were buried. (Genesis 35:29; 47:28-31; 49:29-33; 50:13) At the present time a mosque is built on the site and is regarded as a sacred shrine.

MAHANAIM (ma-ha-na'im) The name given to a place east of the Jordan River by Jacob when he met an angel of the Lord just after he left Laban. (Genesis 32:1-2) It formed part of the boundary between the tribes of Gad and Manasseh, (Joshua 13:26-30) and became a Levitical city. (Joshua 21:38; I Chronicles 6:80) It later became a fortified city and the capital of Ishbosheth, Saul's son. (II Samuel 2:8-9) David sought refuge from Absalom here when Absalom was in possession of Jerusalem. (II Samuel 17:24,27) Here he received the news of Absalom's death. (II Samuel 18:9-33) Barzillai, the Gileadite, was a resident of Mahanaim. He befriended David for which David ordered that his sons would eat at the royal table. (II Samuel 19:32; I Kings 2:7)

Absalom's Death
II SAMUEL 18: 9-17

MAMRE (mam're) A town or district in Hebron where Abraham resided at different times. (Genesis 13:18, 14:13) In this place Abraham entertained three angels of the Lord and was promised a son. (Genesis 18:1,10,14) The cave of Machpelah lay close to Mamre.

MANASSEH Upon request, a half of the tribe of Manasseh received territory on the east side of the Jordan River, along with Reuben and Gad, under the condition that they would assist in expelling the Canaanites on the west side of the river. The other half received lands in the central part of Palestine. (Joshua 13:29-32; 17:5-10) This tribe numbered about 32,000 men of war during the first census, (Numbers 1:36-37) but 38 years later it had grown to over 52,000. (Numbers 26:34) Gideon was from the tribe of Manasseh.

MARAH A fountain in the wilderness of Shur. The children of Israel camped here, about three days after crossing the Red Sea upon leaving Egypt. They found the water bitter and complained to Moses. The Lord directed him to cast a tree into the water and it became sweet. (Exodus 15:23-25; Numbers 33:8)

MEDIA   A country in Asia lying south of the Caspian Sea and west of Parthia. Elam lay to the south and the Zagros mountains to the west. Most of the area was a table land lying 3,000 ft. above sea level. It was known for its fine breed of horses. When Israel was carried into captivity by the Assyrians some of them were placed in the cities of the Medes. (II Kings 17:6; 18:11) Daniel, interpreting Belshazzar's dream, foretold the fall of the Chaldeans to Media. This was carried out shortly thereafter when Darius took the kingdom. (Daniel 5:25-31) Medes were present in Jerusalem on the first day of Pentecost. (Acts 2:9)

MEDITERRANEAN SEA (med-i-terra'n-ean)   The sea lying between Europe and Africa. In Scripture it is referred to as the Sea, or Great Sea. (Numbers 13:29, 34:6; Acts 10:6) or the Hinder or Western Sea. (Deuteronomy 11:24; Joel 2:20) and the sea of the Philistines. (Exodus 23:31) The name Mediterranean was applied at a later date.

MEGIDDO (me-gid'do)   A town of importance in Palestine located in the southern part of the plain of Esdraelon. It was one of the royal cities of Canaan whose king was conquered by Joshua and the Israelites. (Joshua 12:21) It was first assigned to the tribe of Issachar and later to the Manassites, who failed to drive out the inhabitants. (Joshua 17:11-13; Judges 1:27) At the time of Solomon it was firmly occupied by the Israelites and Solomon appointed one of its officers as his commissary. (I Kings 4:12) He also strengthened the fortifications. (I Kings 9:15) King Ahaziah fled from Jehu to Megiddo and was slain there. (II Kings 9:27) Josiah was also slain in Megiddo in a battle against Pharaoh-nechoh, king of Egypt. (II Kings 23:29) The name enters into the composition of Armageddon. (Revelation 16:16) Extensive and important excavations have been made at the city of Megiddo in recent years.

MELITA (mel'ita)   The island in the Mediterranean Sea where Paul was shipwrecked when he journeyed to Rome as a prisoner. He remained there three months, gaining the confidence of the people by healing the sick. (Acts 27:39 to 28-11) It is the island which in all probability is now known as Malta.

MEMPHIS   An important ancient Egyptian capital situated on the delta of the Nile River about 10 miles north of Cairo. In Isaiah and Jeremiah it is referred to as Noph. (Isaiah 19:13; Jeremiah 2:16; 46:14-19)

Paul is shipwrecked   ACTS 27: 39-44

MERIBAH (mer'i-bah)   A name given to a place where the Israelites murmured for lack of water. (Exodus 17:7)

MESOPOTAMIA (mes·o·po·ta′mi·a) The Greek name for the country lying between the Euphrates and Tigris Rivers. The upper region is hilly and fertile, but the lower area near the Tigris is a desert. Nahor lived in this region for a time. Abraham sent his servants here to find a wife for Isaac. (Genesis 24:7-28) Because of their wickedness after the death of Joshua, the Israelites were oppressed for eight years by Chushanrishathaim, king of Mesopotamia and then delivered from their oppression by Othniel. (Judges 3:8-10) Inhabitants of Mesopotamia were present in Jerusalem on Pentecost. (Acts 2:9) Stephen speaks of the Ur of the Chaldees, where Abraham spent his early life, as being in Mesopotamia. (Acts 7:2-4)

Rebekah gave Abraham's servant a drink from her pitcher.　GENESIS 24: 1-28

MICHMASH A town of Benjamin southeast of Bethel and north of Gibeah on the road to Jerusalem. Saul with two thousand men encamped at Michmash to fight the Philistines. Jonathan with one thousand smote the garrison of the Philistines at nearby Gibeah. To avenge themselves, the Philistines gathered a large army with thirty thousand chariots and six thousand horsemen near Michmash. The Israelites fled in terror. Saul retreated to Gilgal where he attempted to rally the Israelites. Here in fear and impatience he offered a burnt offering himself in place of Samuel, for which he was punished. (I Samuel 13:9-14) Jonathan and his army then attacked the Philistines and gained a great victory at Michmash. (I Samuel 14:1-32) Some of the exiles returned to Michmash after the captivity. (Ezra 2:27; Neh. 7:31; 11:31)

MIDIAN A desert region on the northeast coast of the Red Sea. Midian was a son of Abraham by Keturah. (Genesis 25:2-6) Joseph was sold to Midianite merchants who took him to Egypt. (Genesis 37;28,36) After killing the Egyptian, Moses fled to Midian where he married Zipporah and for forty years kept the flocks of his father-in-law, Jethro, the priest of Midian. (Exodus 2:15; 2:21, 3:1; Acts 7:29) The elders of Midian and Moab hired Balaam to curse the Israelites and seduce them to idolatry. (Numbers 22:4-7) As a result the Lord directed Moses to make war on

Joseph sold by his brothers
GENESIS 37: 28-36

them. (Numbers 31) During the time of the judges the Israelites were oppressed by the Midianites for seven years because of their wickedness, and then delivered from oppression by Gideon. (Judges 6; Isaiah 9:4; 10:26)

MILETUS (mi·le′tus)   A seaport and leading city of Ionia, lying about 36 miles south of Ephesus. It had the celebrated temple of Apollo, and the people were immoral. Paul, on his way to Jerusalem on his third missionary journey, stopped at Miletus where he summoned the elders of the church at Ephesus to bid them farewell. (Acts 20:15-38)

MIZPAH (Mizpeh)   1. A heap of stones raised by Jacob as a witness of the covenant made between him and Laban. They made a pact not to pass by that place to do harm to one another. Laban called it Jegarsahadutha and Jacob called it Galeed according to their own language, each meant the same. (Genesis 31:43-55) It was located in Gilead, east of the Jordan River. 2. A town in Gilead east of the Jordan River, also called Ramoth-Gilead. It was the home of Jephthah. (Judges 11:34) He made a vow that if he was victorious over the Ammonites, whosoever would greet him first as he returned home he would offer as a burnt offering. His daughter greeted him and he fulfilled his vow.

Jacob and Laban make a covenant
GENESIS 31: 44-49

(Judges 11:29-40) It was in the territory of Gad, (Joshua 13:26) and was made a Levitical city. (Joshua 21:38) It was here that Jehoshaphat and Ahab battled with Syria to regain the city, and Ahab was slain. (I Kings 22:3-37) Here also Ahaziah and Joram battled against Hazael, king of Syria, and Joram was wounded. (II Ki. 8:28-29) 3. A town of Benjamin. (Joshua 18:26) The tribes of Israel were summoned to Mizpah at times for conference and Samuel judged the people from here. (I Samuel 7:5-17; 10:17; Judges 20:1-3; 21:1,5,8) It was fortified by Asa as a defense against the northern tribes after the division of the kingdom. (I Kings 15:22; II Chronicles 16:6) After Jerusalem was taken by Babylon, Gedaliah was made ruler and he took up residence in Mizpah. (II Kings 25:23-25; Jeremiah 40:6) He was slain by Ishmael. (Jeremiah 41:2-18) It was reoccupied after the captivity and the people helped build the walls of Jerusalem. (Nehemiah 3:7,15,19)

MOAB   A plateau country adapted for grazing with an elevation of about 3,200 ft. occupied by the descendants of Moab, Lot's son. (Genesis 19:39) It is east of the Red Sea with Edom to the south, the river Arnon to the north and the desert to the east. (Numbers 21:11)

*Moab
and surrounding area*

The western border descends abruptly to the Dead Sea, and the shore is fertile, fed by springs. Coming up from Egypt, the Israelites requested permission from the Moabites to pass through their land to reach Canaan, but being refused they went around its borders. (Judges 11:17-18) Moses was forbidden by God to attack the Moabites. (Deuteronomy 2:9) Balaak, king of Moab, alarmed when the Israelites camped near Moab, because the Israelites had overcome the Amorites, sent for Balaam to come and curse them. (Numbers 22,23,24) For this the Moabites were excluded from the congregation to the tenth generation and treated with indifference by Israel forever. (Deuteronomy 23:3-6; Nehemiah 13:1) During a famine, Elimelech lived in Moab, as did Ruth and Orpha, his daughters-in-law. (Ruth 1:1-4)

MOREH, THE PLAINS OF   The first recorded place where Abraham stopped in Canaan after leaving Haran, when God told him to leave his country and go to Canaan. (Genesis 12:6) Here God promised him and his seed all the land of Canaan and Abraham built an altar unto the Lord. (Genesis 12:7-8)

MORIAH   1. The land in which Abraham was to offer up Isaac as a sacrifice. (Genesis 22:2) 2. The hill on which the threshing floor of Ornan, or Araunah, the Jebusite was located. David purchased the floor and built an altar on it. (II Samuel 24:18-25) Solomon built the temple on this site. (II Chronicles 3:1) It was located between the Kidron and Tyropoeon Valleys.

MOSERAH   An encampment of the Israelites in the wilderness. Aaron died and was buried here. (Deuteronomy 10:6) The exact site is not known, but it was near Mount Hor by the border of Edom. (Numbers 20:23-29)

God tests Abraham's faith when He asks him to sacrifice Isaac. GENESIS 22: 1-14

MYRA   One of the principal cities of Lycia. It was a seaport on the Mediterranean Sea, and a place where Paul changed ships as a prisoner on his way to Rome. (Acts 27:5-6)

MYSIA   A district in the northwest part of Asia Minor, separated from Europe by the straits of Hellespont and Protontis. Paul passed through Mysia on his way to Troas, one of its principal cities, where he received a vision urging him to come to Macedonia to preach the Gospel. (Acts 16:7-10)

N

NAIN   A village in Galilee at the gate of which Jesus raised a widow's son from the dead. (Luke 7:11-16)

NAPHTALI   This was one of the last of the tribes to receive its territory in the drawing of lots. It was given an area in the northern portion of the country

Raising the widow's son   LUKE 19: 41

bordering on the Jordan River to the east and by the tribe of Zebulun and Asher on the west. (Joshua 19:32-35) The tribe numbered 53,000 men in the first census taken in the wilderness. (Numbers 1:42-43) One of its leaders was Barak, who at the command of Deborah gathered an army of 10,000 men and destroyed the enemy. (Judges 4:1-24)

NAZARETH A town lying in a valley in lower Galilee a little north of the plain of Esdraelon. It is not mentioned in the O. T. Joseph and Mary lived in Nazareth, (Luke 2:39) and it is where the angel Gabriel announced to Mary that she was to be the mother of Jesus. (Luke 1:26-35) Joseph brought Mary and the young child Jesus to Nazareth after leaving Egypt, and Jesus spent His childhood here. (Matthew 2:19-23) Later He taught in the synagogue. (Luke 4:16) He was known as Jesus of Nazareth because of His long association with this town. (Luke 18:37; 24:19; John 1:45; Acts 2:22)

The boy Jesus in the carpenter shop

NEAPOLIS A seaport ten miles from Philippi in Macedonia visited by Paul on his first missionary journey to Europe. (Acts 16:11)

NEBO The peak or summit of Mount Pisgah near Jericho from which Moses viewed the promised land. (Deuteronomy 32:49; 34:1) Here Moses died and was buried by God in a valley in the land of Moab. (Deuteronomy 34:5-6)

NILE The great river of Egypt. It runs from south to north through a large expanse of desert in northern Africa, emptying into the Mediterranean Sea. It gave to Egypt the water necessary for its very existence. The annual inundation of the Nile brought deposits of rich soil to make agriculture possible along its banks. It provided the chief means of transportation and communication as well as game and fowl among the brush, and its papyrus plant furnished the writing material. Although not mentioned by name, the Nile is often referred to in Scripture. As a baby, Moses was put in a basket by his mother and placed in the river Nile to

Pharaoh's daughter finds baby Moses.

EXODUS 2: 3-10

save him from the tyranny of Pharaoh. (Exodus 2:3) In one of the plagues prior to the Exodus the waters of the Nile were turned to blood. (Exodus 7:20) Isaiah refers to it when he prophesied the confusion of Egypt. (Isaiah 19:5)

NINEVEH The ancient capital city of Assyria, situated on the eastern bank of the Tigris River. It was built by people of Babylonian origin. (Genesis 10:11) Nineveh became a beautiful city with splendid temples and palaces, and was fortified with high walls. It was a wicked city and its rulers were cruel and bloody, because of which, the prophets foretold of its destruction. (Nehemiah 2 and 3) Jonah was directed by God to go to Nineveh to preach

Jonah is cast out of the mouth of the fish.
JONAH 1: 11-2: 10

repentance to its people. He tried to flee from God and was swallowed by a large fish. After he was free, God again told him to go. He went and preached, and many heeded his words. (Jonah 1,2,3,4) The city was destroyed in 612 B.C by Medes, Babylonians and Scythians, and was not heard of again until recent excavations have found some parts of it.

NOB A town in the terriory of Benjamin a short distance from Jerusalem. (Nehemiah 11:32; Isaiah 10:32) The Ark of the Covenant was placed in Nob for a time before David had it moved to Jerusalem. In Nob, David applied to the high priest Ahimelech for bread after he fled from Saul. (I Samuel 21:1-5) Unaware of the conflict between David and Saul, he gave David holy bread and Goliath's sword. Saul, when he heard of this, had the priest and all the inhabitants of Nob slain, except for Abiathar who escaped and told David of the incident. (I Samuel 21 and 22) It was reinhabited after the Babylonian exile. (Nehemiah 11:32)

NOD A place on the east of Eden to which Cain fled after the murder of Abel. (Genesis 4:16)

O

OLIVES, MOUNT OF — also Olivet A ridge of hills east of Jerusalem, separated from it by the valley of Kidron. (II Samuel 15:14,23,30) It is composed of limestone and is about one mile in length, running north and south. At its northern end it bends to the west encompassing the north side of the city. Jesus often went to the Mount of Olives to teach, (Matthew 24:3; 26:30; Mark 13:3; 14:26; John 8:1) and to pray. (Luke 22:39) He descended the mount coming from Bethany on His triumphal entry into Jerusalem. (Mark 11:1; Luke 19:37) Here He wept over Jerusalem and predicted its

Jesus weeping over Jerusalem
LUKE 19: 41

destruction. (Luke 19:37-44) Zechariah prophesied Jehovah standing on the mount at the destruction of Jerusalem, intervening in behalf of His people. (Zechariah 14:4) The Garden of Gethsemane was located at the foot of the Mount of Olives.

ON   An old and famous city of lower Egypt. It was the center for the worship of the sun god, Ra. Pharaoh gave to Joseph, Asenath, daughter of a priest of On, for a wife. (Genesis 41:45,50; 46:20)

P

PALESTINE   The modern name for an area in southwestern Asia. Originally it was called Philistia. After the sojourn in Egypt, it roughly designated the territory comparable to the land of Canaan or the promised land, also the United Kingdom of Israel. It lies between the Mediterranean Sea and the desert east of the Jordan River. The southern boundary was in the area of Beersheba and the northern boundary at Mount Hermon. The area generally occupied by the Hebrews was approximately 8,300 square miles, which is comparable in size to the state of Massachusetts. The geography of Palestine is varied and includes the maritime plain along the Mediterranean Sea, the central mountain range having an average height of about 2,000 ft., and the Jordan Valley and eastern Palestine which is a large fertile plateau east of the Jordan River. Because of the varied elevation, the climate differs in the various parts of the country. It has two seasons, winter, which is rainy and mild from November to April, and summer, which is hot and dry from May to October. The history of Palestine is written throughout the Old Testament, beginning in Genesis. (Genesis 10:15-19) Following the wanderings in the wilderness the

Jesus the Good Shepherd
JOHN 10: 11-18

people of Israel possessed the land then known as Canaan under the leadership of Joshua. After the exile, they again returned to occupy the land. Palestine was the area in which Jesus carried out His ministry.

PAMPHYLIA (pamphyl'i-a)   A narrow coastal region on the Mediterranean Sea in Asia Minor. It was bounded on the north by Pisidia, on the east by Cilicia and on the west by Lycia. Jews residing in Pamphylia were present in Jerusalem at the first Pentecost. (Acts 2:10) Paul visited two of its cities, Perga and Attalia on his first missionary journey. (Acts 13:13; 14:24-25; 15:38)

PAPHOS   A town at the southwest end of Cyprus. Paul, on his first missionary journey, came to Paphos where he met Elymas (Barjesus), the sorcerer, whom he struck with temporary blindness for trying to turn away the faith of a Roman deputy. (Acts 13:6-12)

PARAN (pa'ran)   A wilderness south of Canaan and north of Sinai which apparently contained the wilderness of Sin. Ishmael dwelt in Paran. (Genesis 21:21) After leaving Sinai, the Israelites camped here, (Numbers 10:12;12:16) and from here Moses sent spies to Canaan to search the land. (Numbers 13:1-33) David sought refuge from Saul in Paran after the death of Samuel. (I Samuel 25:1)

PARTHIA   A country that was first mentioned in about 521 B.C. It was situated in the vicinity of the Euphrates and Tigris Rivers, and encompassed what had been parts of Assyria and Babylonia. Jews from Parthia were present in Jerusalem at the first Pentecost. (Acts 2:9)

PATMOS   An island off the southwestern coast of Asia Minor. It was a rocky, barren, desolate place used by the Roman government as a place of banishment for criminals. John was sent here for testifying of Jesus Christ and here he saw the visions recorded in the Book of Revelation. (Revelation 1:9)

PENUEL   A place east of the Jordan River and north of the brook Jabbok, so named by Jacob because he had wrestled with God and his name was changed from Jacob to Israel. (Genesis 32:24-32) Gideon destroyed the towers of Penuel because the men refused to give bread to his army. (Judges 8:8,9,17) Jeroboam later fortified it. (I Kings 12:25) Once called Peniel.

PERGA   The capital of the province Pamphylia in Asia Minor. It was visited by Paul and Barnabas on their first missionary journey. (Acts 13:13-14)

PERSIA   A world empire which flourished from 539-331 B.C. Cyrus II founded the mighty Persian Empire in 559 B.C. and its supremacy grew rapidly, surpassing that of Media and Elam. Persia was a great mountainous plateau east of the lower end of the Euphrates-Tigris Valley. The Persian Empire extended eastward to the borders of India and westward to Greece. Cyrus, king of Persia, was a humane leader who issued the decree restoring the Jews to their homeland after the surrender of Babylon to Persia. (II Chronicles 36:22-23; Ezra 1:2-3) Both Ezra and Nehemiah were prominent in the return from captivity (Ezra; Nehemiah) In 331 B.C. the empire fell to the conquests of Alexander the Great.

PHILADELPHIA   A city in the province of Lydia in Asia Minor located about 27 miles southeast of Sardis. It was destroyed by an earthquake in 17 A.D., was rebuilt and became the seat of one of the seven churches of Asia addressed in the Book of Revelation. (Revelation 1:11; 3:7-13)

PHILIPPI (phi-lip'pi)   A city of Macedonia, originally known as Krenides. King Philip took it from the Thracians and gave it his own name. It was situated about 10 miles from the Aegean Sea and the port of Neapolis. Paul with Silas visited Philippi on the second missionary journey when Lydia and her household, a girl possessed with an evil spirit and the Philippian jailer were converted. (Acts 16:12-40) Paul had to leave Philippi but returned later from whence he sailed to Troas. (Acts 20:6) The Philippians were the first among the Macedonians to be converted to Christianity. (Philippians 4:15)

Lydia opened her home to Paul. ACTS 16: 14-15

PHILISTIA (phi-list′i-a)   A country settled by a powerful seafaring people in Canaan, extending along the coast of the Mediterranean from Joppa to south of Gaza. The five principal cities of Philistia were Gaza, Ashkelon, Ashdod, Gath and Ekron. The Philistines had a warlike nature and were a natural enemy of the Israelites. They were left by the Lord to prove the Israelites, (Judges 3:3-4) and many battles ensued during which the Ark of the Covenant was carried away. Jonathan defeated the Philistines at Michmash. (I Samuel 13 and 14)   David also won victories over them, (I Samuel 17 and 18) and during the reigns of David and Solomon they were completely subjugated. They disappeared from history after the Babylonian conquest.

PHOENICIA (phoe-ni′ci-a)   A narrow coastal country along the northeastern Mediterranean shore. Its principal cities were Tyre and Sidon. The name Palestine came from the Greeks through Phoenicia. The Phoenicians were a seagoing people trading with distant countries. Jesus visited Tyre and Sidon where He healed the daughter of a woman of great faith. (Matthew 15:21-28; Mark 7:24-31) Christians went to Phoenicia after the persecution of Stephen. (Acts 11:19) Paul and Barnabas passed through it on their way from Antioch to Jerusalem. (Acts 15:3) Paul on his last voyage sailed on a Phoenician vessel which brought him to Tyre. (Acts 21:2-3)

PHRYGIA (phryg′i-a)   A province of Asia Minor. Four of its cities mentioned in the New Testament were Laodicea, Collossae, Antioch of Pisidia, and Hierapolis. The country was fertile and its rich pastures made it famous for its fine breed of cattle. Paul visited this province twice on his missionary journeys. (Acts 16:6; 18:23) Jews from Phrygia were in Jerusalem on the day of the first Pentecost. (Acts 2:10)

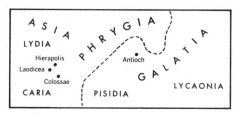

Phrygia and adjoining provinces

PISGAH   A mountain which lies near the northeast side of the Dead Sea. It was here that Balak built seven altars when he had asked Balaam to curse the Israelites.

(Numbers 22,23,24)   Moses viewed the promised land from its summit which is Nebo. (Deuteronomy 3:27, 34:1-4)

PISIDIA   A district in Asia Minor, north of Pamphylia. In New Testament times it formed part of the province of Galatia. Antioch was its chief city, however it is to be distinguished from the more renowned Antioch of Syria. Paul visited here twice, preaching the Gospel. (Acts 13:14; 14:21-24)

PONTUS   A large district in Asia Minor in the southern coastal region of the Black Sea. People from here were present in Jerusalem at the first Pentecost. (Acts 2:9) Aquila was a native of Pontus. (Acts 18:2) Christians here were named in the salutation of the first epistle of Peter (1 Peter 1:1)

R

RABBAH   A chief city of the Ammonites, located east of the Jordan River at the headwaters of the Jabbok River. Joab, head of David's army, fought against Rabbah, and it was during one of these battles that Uriah, the Hittite, husband of Bathsheba, was killed. (II Samuel 11:2-17)   David completed the conquest of the city and the people were put in bondage. (II Samuel 12:26-31; I Chronicles 20:1-3) In time the Ammonites recovered the city and judgments were pronounced against it by Jeremiah, Ezekiel and Amos. (Jeremiah 49:2; Ezekiel 21:20; 25:5; Amos 1:14)

RAMAH   Several places in Palestine were called Ramah, meaning "the height." These were places located on a hill for the purpose of safety. **1.** A town in Benjamin just north of Jerusalem, near Gibeah, Geba and Bethel. (Joshua 18:25; Judges 4:5; 19:13-14; Isaiah 10:29) It was fortified by Baasha, king of Israel. (I Kings 15:17-22; II Chronicles 16:1-6) It was reoccupied after the captivity. (Ezra 2:26; Nehemiah 11:33) **2.** The town where Samuel's parents lived and where he was born and made his residence. (I Samuel 1:19; 2:11; 7:17; 8:4; 15:34; 16:13; 19:18) Samuel was buried in Ramah. (I Samuel 25:1; 28:3)

RAMESES   (see Goshen)

RED SEA   A long narrow body of water about 1,490 miles in length, extending from the Indian Ocean to the Suez Gulf, forming the boundary between Egypt and Arabia. God allowed the children of Israel to cross the Red Sea by holding back the waters. The pursuing Egyptians were destroyed as the waters returned. (Exodus 14:26-30; 15:4,22) It is believed that this crossing took place at the

Parting of the waters   EXODUS 14: 27

northern end at a point now known as Bitter Lakes, which in those days were probably part of the Red Sea.

REPHAIM (repha'-im) A fertile valley near Bethlehem, southwest of Jeru-salem and the valley of Hinnom. It was the scene of the approach of the Philistines as they sought David, and featured in two conflicts in which he defeated them. (II Samuel 5:18-22; 23:13-14; I Chronicles 11:15; 14:9-17)

REPHIDIM (reph'i-dim) A camping ground of the Israelites as they jour-neyed from the wilderness of Sin to Mount Sinai. (Numbers 33:14-15)

Moses striking rock for water

NUMBERS 20: 7-12

Because of lack of water, they murmured to Moses. By divine command, he struck the rock at Horeb and obtained an abundance of water. (Exodus 17:1-8; 19:2) Rephidim was the scene of a battle between Amalek and the children of Israel. (Exodus 17:8-16) (see Jehovahnissi)

REUBEN The tribe of Reuben along with Gad and the half tribe of Manasseh asked Moses for lands east of the Jordan River. They had many cattle and flocks of sheep and these lands were especially suitable for their needs. Reuben was assigned an area east of the Dead Sea in the country formerly occupied by the Ammonites. (Joshua 13:15-21) The tribe numbered 46,000 male adults. (Numbers 1:20-21)

ROMAN EMPIRE Originally a strip of land surrounded by the Mediterranean Sea, founded by Romulus in 753 B.C. Its capital city was Rome situated on the Tiber River. The kingdom grew in size and importance through the reign of seven kings. The tyranny of one of their kings drove the people to revolt, and they formed a republic. During the period of the republic, its boundaries were extended over all of Italy and finally over the whole known world. Judea became subject to the Roman Empire in 63 B.C., and although it had its own rulers it was required to pay tribute to the Romans. It was in the reign of Augustus that Christ was born, and during the reign of Tiberius that the crucifixion took place. In its height, the empire extended 2,000 miles from north to south and 3,000 miles from east to west, containing a population of about 120,000,000 people. Through corruption within and attack without, the empire began to decline until it was captured by the Goth, Odoacer in 476. The religion of the Roman Empire was pagan although under its rule Christianity was tolerated, but nonetheless persecuted. Under Constantine in the fourth century, Christianity was declared the religion of the state. Romans were present in Jerusalem at the first Pentecost. (Acts 2:10) Aquila and Priscilla spent some time in Rome until all Jews were commanded to leave. (Acts 18:2) Paul, as a prisoner, sailed to Rome. (Acts 28:14-31) He wrote the epistle to the Romans to the Christians in Rome. (Romans 1:1-7)

S

SALAMIS   A city on the east coast of Cyprus. Paul preached here in the synagogues on his first missionary journey. (Acts 13:4-5)

SALT, VALLEY OF   A valley at the southern end of the Dead Sea. David's army slew 18,000 men in this valley. (II Samuel 8:13; I Chronicles 18:12) and Amaziah, king of Judah, smote 10,000 children of Seir. (Edomites) (II Chronicles 25:11; II Kings 14:7)

SALT SEA   (see Dead Sea)

SAMARIA   1. The capital city of the ten tribes comprising the northern kingdom. It was located on a hill in central Palestine. (I Kings 16:24; II Kings 3:1) From its very beginning under Omri it was notorious for idolatry. King Ahab had altars built for Baal and heathenism prevailed until the northern kingdom was captured by the Assyrians. (I Kings 16:32; Jeremiah 23:13-14; Ezekiel 16:46-55; Amos 6:1; Micah 1:1) Jehu broke down the temples of Baal but idol worship continued. (II Kings 10:17-31) The city was twice besieged by the Syrians, about 863 B.C. (I Kings 20:1) and

Jesus and the Samaritan woman
JOHN 4: 4-26

again around 843 B.C. (II Kings 6:24) It was finally taken in 721 B.C. by the Assyrians when the northern kingdom was destroyed. (II Kings 18:9-12) Samaria was the scene of the ministry of the prophets Elijah and Elisha.
2. In New Testament times the district occupying central Palestine between Galilee on the north and Judea on the south. It was here in the city of Sychar that Jesus met the Samaritan woman at Jacob's well (John 4:4-30)

SARDIS   A city of wealth in western Asia Minor about 50 miles east of Smyrna. It was the fifth city named of the seven churches addressed by John. (Revelation 1:11; 3:1-4)

SELEUCIA   A seaport on the coast of Syria with an excellent harbor, north of the Orontes River. It served as the seaport for Antioch. Paul and Barnabas sailed from Seleucia for Cyprus on Paul's first missionary journey. (Acts 13:4)

SEPULCHERS OF THE KINGS   The royal burial place in the city of David, near the king's garden and the pool of Shelah. (I Kings 2:10; II Chronicles 21:20; Nehemiah 3:15-16) All the kings from David through Hezekiah were buried in the city of David and the royal sepulcher was ordinarily used, although Asa and Hezekiah had their own tombs. (II Chronicles 16:13-14; 32:33) Jehoram, Joash, Uzziah and Ahaz were not admitted to the royal sepulcher. (II Chronicles 21:20; 24:25; 26:23; 28:27)

SHECHEM   An ancient city in Palestine where Abraham camped after leaving Haran. He found Canaanites living there, but knowing this was the land that God had promised him he built an altar. (Genesis 12:6-8) Jacob also came to Shechem and found Hivites living in the area. He bought a parcel of ground from them and built an altar of the Lord. (Genesis 33:18-20) Jacob and his family lived in harmony with the Hivites and his sons fed their flocks in Shechem for a time. (Genesis 37:12- 13) The boundary between the tribes of Ephraim and Manasseh passed near here. (Joshua 17:7) It became a Levitical city and a city of refuge. (Joshua 20:7; 21:21) It was here that Joshua gave his farewell address to the tribes of Israel. (Joshua 24:1) Joseph's body was brought to Shechem for burial. (Joshua 24:32) Abimelech, for a time, gained followers in Shechem but later he was rejected and he destroyed the town. (Judges 9:1-57) It was at Shechem that the northern tribes rejected Rehoboam and made Jeroboam their king. It was fortified and became his capital city. (I Kings 12:1- 25) Shechem was located on the side of Mount Gerizim north of Jerusalem.

SHILOH A town north of Bethel within the boundary of Ephraim. (Judges 21:19) Here the Israelites, under Joshua, set up the tabernacle with the Ark of the Covenant and divided by lot the unappropriated parts of Canaan. (Joshua 18:10) The tabernacle remained in Shiloh up to the time of Eli and the early years of Samuel. (Judges 18:31; I Samuel 1:9,24; 2:14,22; 3:3,21; 4:3-4) The ark was carried off by the Philistines when they defeated Israel at Shiloh. (I Samuel 4; Jeremiah 7:12-14; 26:6,9) Ahijah lived in Shiloh. It was he who told Jeroboam that he would be king over the ten tribes. (I Kings 11:31) When their child became ill, Jeroboam's wife went

Hannah leaves young Samuel with Eli in the house of the Lord. I SAMUEL 1: 24-28

to this town to inquire of the prophet what would become of the child. (I Kings 14:1-18)

SHITTIM An important encampment of the Israelites east of the Jordan River near Jericho, in the plains of Moab. (Numbers 22:1 with 25:1) It was here that Moses delivered his farewell address, (Deuteronomy) and charged Joshua to lead the people into the promised land. (Deuteronomy 31:1-8) The Israelites camped here before invading Canaan and from here Joshua sent two spies to view Jericho and the surrounding lands. (Joshua 2:1-24; 3:1)

SHUNEM A town in Canaan near Mount Carmel. It was the home of the Shunammite woman who invited the prophet Elisha to eat in her home whenever he passed by. Later she had a special chamber built for the prophet on the wall of their house. When her son became ill and died, she sent for Elisha who prayed to the Lord and the child was restored to life. (II Kings 4:8-37)

SHUR A wilderness area east of Egypt beyond the Red Sea and south of the land of Canaan. It was here that Hagar was found by the angel of the Lord, after fleeing from Sarah, the wife of Abraham. (Genesis 16:9-14) The Israelites marched through this wilderness for three days after departing from Egypt. (Exodus 15:22)

SHUSHAN   The capital city and royal residence of the Persian kings. Esther became queen when Vashti fell from the favor of King Ahasuerus. (Esther Ch. 1 & 2)

SIDON OR ZIDON   An ancient Phoenician city located about twenty miles north of Tyre. It was the capital city, located on the Mediterranean Sea. (Genesis 10:15,19) Ethbaal, king of Sidon, was the father of Jezebel. (I Kings 16:31)   Baalim and Ashtaroth were the heathen gods of this city. (Judges 10:6)   Sidon was denounced by the prophets. (Isaiah 23:2,4; Jeremiah 27:3; Ezekiel 28:21)   It was in this area that Jesus encountered the woman of Canaan, healed her daughter and praised her for her great faith. (Matthew 15:21-28)

SILOAM   A pool at Jerusalem. Jesus commanded the man blind from birth to wash in the pool and he gained his sight. (John 9:7)

SIMEON   One of the larger tribes which was given its land in the southernmost part of Canaan, partly within the area given to Judah. (Joshua 19:1-9) The two tribes joined together to drive out the Canaanites. (Judges 1:3,17)

SIN   A wilderness through which the Israelites passed on their way from Egypt to the promised land. It was located between Elim and Sinai. (Exodus 16:1) Manna was first given to the Israelites in the wilderness of Sin. (Exodus 16:2-18)

SINAI, MOUNT OF   A mountain, also called Horeb, in the wilderness through which the Israelites traveled. (Exodus 19:1)   It rises to a height of over 7,000 feet. The ten commandments were given to the Israelites on Mount Sinai. (Exodus 20:1-17)   Elijah visited this mountain after he was threatened by Jezebel. (I Kings 19:8) (see Horeb)

The children of Israel gather bread from heaven.   EXODUS 16: 11-21

SMYRNA   An ancient city on the western coast of Asia Minor, which was destroyed by Alyattes, the Lydian king, and lay in ruins for some 200 years. It was rebuilt by the successors of Alexander the Great and became a flourishing center of commerce. John, in the Book of Revelation spoke of Smyrna when he addressed the seven churches. (Rev. 1:11; 2:8-11)

SODOM   A city in the plain of Jordan. (Genesis 13:10)   Lot moved to Sodom when he separated from Abraham even though it was already known for its

Moses with the tablets of Law
EXODUS 20: 1-17

wickedness. (Genesis 13:11-12) Chedor-laomer plundered the city, but Abraham pursued him and recovered both the goods and the captives. (Genesis 14:11-24) Together with Gomorrah, Sodom was destroyed with fire and brimstone by God because of the wickedness of the people. Lot's wife looked back on the burning city and was turned into a pillar of salt. (Genesis 19:24-26)

Lot's wife was turned into a pillar of salt.
GENESIS 19: 24-26

SUCCOTH 1. A town east of the Jordan river. After leaving Esau, Jacob journeyed to Succoth where he built himself a house and booths for his cattle. (Genesis 33:17) It was in the valley of the Jordan where foundries for making brass vessels for the temple were located. (I Kings 7:46; II Chronicles 4:17) The men of Succoth refused to help Gideon when he was pursuing Zebah and Zalmunna, for which he returned to punish them. (Judges 8:5:16)
2. The first encampment of the Israelites after leaving Rameses or Goshen. (Numbers 33:5-6)

SYCHAR A town in Samaria near Jacob's well. (John 4:5-6) It was home of the woman of Samaria of whom Jesus asked a drink. (John 4:7-26)

SYNAGOGUE A place of religious instruction at which the people assembled on the Sabbath for the reading of the Scriptures and prayer. Jesus often taught in the synagogue. (Matthew 4:23; Mark 1:22; 5:22; 6:2; Luke 4:16; 6:6; 13:14) They were found wherever Jews were located. Larger cities had a number of synagogues. In the book of Acts and in Paul's letters, there are many references to Paul teaching in the synagogue. (Acts 13:5; 13:14-15; 14:1; 17:10) It is believed that the synagogue was established after the Babylonian exile.

SYRACUSE An important city on the east coast of Sicily. Paul stopped here for three days on his voyage to Rome. (Acts 28:12)

SYRIA A country north of Palestine bordering on the Mediterranean Sea. Damascus was the capital and Antioch an important city. (I Kings 15-18) This kingdom was often at war with the Israelites and once was allied with Israel against Judah. (I Kings 20:1; II Kings 8:28; 16:5) Syria fell to the Assyrians in 740 B.C., then to the Persians. In New Testament times, it was a province in the

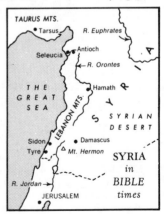

TAURUS MTS.
Tarsus
R. Euphrates
Seleucia
Antioch
R. Orontes
THE GREAT SEA
Hamath
LEBANON MTS.
SYRIAN DESERT
Sidon
Damascus
Tyre
Mt. Hermon
SYRIA
in
R. Jordan
BIBLE
JERUSALEM
times

Roman Empire, with Antioch as its capital. (Matthew 4:24; Luke 2:2; Acts 15:23; Galatians 1:21) The scene of Paul's conversion was on the road to Damascus. (Acts 26:12-18)

T

TABERNACLE The tabernacle was a portable temple or sanctuary which was the center of worship for the Israelites during the wanderings in the wilderness. Directions for its construction were given to Moses on Mount Sinai. (Exodus 25-28) After they entered the promised land, it was placed at Shiloh and during Samuel's time it was apparently transferred to Mizpeh. (I Samuel 7:6) Later it was placed in Gibeon. (I Kings 3:4; I Chronicles 16:39) It remained the center of worship until Solomon's temple was completed. The tabernacle proper was divided into two sections, the Holy of Holies, which housed the Ark of the Covenant, and the Holy Place. The tabernacle, the brazen altar and the laver were surrounded by an enclosed courtyard. (Ex. 25-27)

TABOR A mountain on the plain of Esdraelon about 6 miles east of Nazareth. At the command of Deborah, Barak gathered his forces on Tabor to descend with ten thousand men into the plain to conquer Sisera. (Judges 4:6-15)

TARSUS The capital city of Cilicia and birthplace of Paul. (Acts 9:11; 21:39; 22:3) He revisited it after his conversion. (Acts 9:30; 11:25)

TEKOA A fortified town of Judah about six miles south of Bethlehem. (II Chronicles 20:20) Joab employed a "wise woman" of Tekoa to effect a reconciliation between David and Absalom. (II Samuel 14:1-23) It was fortified by Rehoboam to prevent invasion from the south. (II Chronicles 11:5-6) Here Amos made his home when he was called to be a prophet. (Amos 1:1)

TEMPLE A worship center dedicated to God. **1. Solomon's Temple.** Planned by David as a permanent house of the Lord in Jerusalem to replace the tabernacle. (I Chronicles 28:2) He received the plans from God and gathered much of the material necessary, but was not allowed to build it because of his background as a man of war. (I Chronicles 22:8; 28:3) The task was given to his son, Solomon. (II Samuel 7:9-13; I Kings 5:3-4; I Chronicles 22:7-17) The temple was built on Mount Moriah. It was begun in 960 B.C., and completed in 7½ years. (I Kings 6:1) The general plan was like the tabernacle, but the dimensions were double and it was far more ornate. The

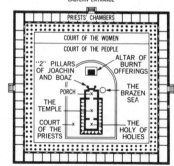

Plan of Solomon's Temple showing the two inner courts.

58

interior measured 60 cubits in length, 20 in breadth and 30 in height. The walls were made of stone and lined with cedar. The roof was also of cedar and the floors of cypress. The interior was lined with gold and covered with carvings. The temple was divided into two rooms as was the tabernacle. The Holy of Holies was a cube with each dimension being 20 cubits. It housed the Ark which was placed under two large cherubims. The holy place or sanctuary measured 40 cubits long, 20 wide and 30 high. It contained the altar of incense, 10 golden candlesticks and 10 tables.

In addition to the temple proper there was a building housing the officials. The temple area also contained two courts — the inner being the court of the priests and the great or outer court was for Israel. They were separated from each other by a low wall. The court of the priests contained the brazen altar for sacrifice, the brazen sea for the priests to wash themselves, and the brazen lavers for the washing of utensils. (I Kings 6 & 7) Solomon's temple was ransacked and burned, by Nebuchadnezzar when he besieged Jerusalem in 587 B.C. (II Kings 25:8-17)

2. Zerubbabel's Temple After the return of the Jews from captivity, Cyrus authorized the erection of a temple in Jerusalem. (Ezra 6:3) Construction was begun in 537 B.C. which was the second year after their return. The plan in general followed that of Solomon's temple but on a far less elaborate scale. (Ezra 3:12) Many of the vessels from Solomon's temple were restored but the holy of holies was left empty for the

King Hezekiah reopens the doors of the Temple and repairs them.

II CHRONICLES 29: 3-11

Ark of the Covenant had disappeared. Later Zerubbabel's temple was plundered and used for idolatrous purposes.

3. Herod's Temple Work on this temple was begun in 19 B.C. Herod replaced the temple that existed when he began his reign. It was on a grander scale than Zerubbabel's, surrounded by courts. It included an outer court which could be frequented by Gentiles and unclean persons, the women's court, and the inner court, which contained the chambers for storing the utensils and entered onto the priest's court. The temple proper stood higher than the courts and was approached by a flight of twelve steps. It contained the Holy of Holies and the Holy Place. A veil separated the two. It was this veil that was rent on the occasion of Jesus' crucifixion. (Matthew 27:51; Mark 15:38; Luke 23:45)

THESSALONICA (thes-sa-lo-ni'ca) An important city of Macedonia. On his second missionary journey, Paul came here with Silas, preached in the synagogue and made many converts for the Gospel, who became the nucleus of a Christian church. (Acts 17:1-13) Paul later sent two letters to the church in Thessalonica. It was the home of two of his co-workers, Aristarchus and Secundus. (Acts 20:4)

THYATIRA (thy-a-ti′ra) A city in Lydia of Asia Minor. Lydia, the seller of purple in Philippi, came from Thyatira. (Acts 16:14) One of the seven churches referred to in Revelations was located here. (Revelation 1:11; 2:18-24)

TIBERIAS A city on the Sea of Galilee at the time of Christ. (John 6:23) Also another name for the Sea of Galilee. (John 6:1; 21:1)

TIGRIS (See Hiddekel)

Lydia opened her home to Paul. ACTS 16: 14-15

TIRZAH A city originally belonging to the Canaanites which was captured by Joshua. (Joshua 12:24) It became the capital city of the kingdom of Israel up to the reign of Omri. (I Kings 14:17; 15:21,33; 16:6,8,9,15,17,23)

TOPHETH A location, perhaps a grove, near Jerusalem in the valley of Hinnom, where the deity Molech was worshiped. Children were made to pass through fire as an offering to Molech. (II Kings 23:10; Jeremiah 7:31; 19:5-6) This heathen worship was first practiced by ancient Canaanites and later by apostate Israelites. (II Kings 16:3) Jeremiah prophesied the destruction of Topheth. (Jeremiah 7:32)

TROAS A seaport in the province of Mysia. (Acts 16:11) Paul, while in Troas, saw a vision in which a man of Macedonia invited him to come to Europe to preach the Gospel. (Acts 16:8-10; II Corinthians 2:12) On one occasion Paul remained in Troas seven days. It was here that he brought the young man, Eutychus, back to life after he had fallen asleep while Paul was preaching and fell out of a third floor window. (Acts 20:6-12)

TYRE An ancient Phoenician city located on the Mediterranean Sea. Its wealth and prosperity depended on trade. (Isaiah 23:7-8) Hiram, king of Tyre, was friendly with David and Solomon and assisted in supplying material and labor for the building of David's palace and to Solomon for the building of the temple and other royal buildings. (II Samuel 5:11; I Kings 5:1-11; 9:11-14; I Chronicles 14:1; II Chronicles 2:3-16) When Jesus visited the area of Tyre and Sidon, a woman of Canaan beseeched Him to rid her daughter of the devil. Because of her great faith her daughter was made well. (Matthew 15:21-28; Mark 7:24-31) Christians lived in Tyre during Paul's ministry. (Acts 21:3-6)

U

UR A city of the Chaldees or Babylonia which was the birthplace of Abraham. (Gen. 11:27-28; 15:7; Neh. 9:7) From here he migrated to Haran. (Gen. 11:31)

W

WILDERNESS OF THE WANDERING The region in which the Israelites sojourned and wandered for forty years on their way from Egypt to Canaan. The wilderness was a large inverted triangular area within the Sinai Peninsula. It consisted of several districts: the wilderness of Shur to the north, the wilderness of Paran in the central portion, the wilderness of Sin in the lower part and the wilderness of Zin to the northeast. It was chiefly in the wilderness of Paran that the children of Israel wandered for thirty-eight years. The wilderness did not supply sufficient water and food for the over 2,000,000 people, but God miraculously supplied manna, water and occasionally quail to sustain them. (Exodus 16:1-31,35; 17:3-7) Because of their unbelief and rebellion, God commanded that the Israelites should wander in the wilderness until all who were over 21 years of age should perish. (Numbers 14:32-35) The account of the wanderings in the wilderness is found beginning with Exodus 15:22 and ending with Joshua 3:17. It was in the wilderness at Mount Sinai that God gave His people the ten commandments. (Exodus 19 to 20:17)

Mt. Sinai in the wilderness
EXODUS 19-20:17

Z

ZAREPHATH (zar'e-phath) An ancient Phoenician city lying on the coast between Tyre and Sidon. During the drought and famine, Elijah came here and asked a widow for something to eat and drink. Trusting in the Lord, she gave him a little of what she had. As a reward of her faith her supply of oil and meal never ran out and her son was restored to life. (I Kings 17:9-24; Luke 4:26)

ZARETAN A village near the Jordan River named in connection with the miraculous crossing of the river by the Israelites. (Joshua 3:16) It was between here and Succoth that the bronze work for Solomon's temple was cast. (I Kings 7:46)

ZEBULUN This tribe numbering about 57,000 adult males (Numbers 1:31) was allotted an area in the northern part of the land of Palestine. It bordered both on the

Mediterranean Sea and the Sea of Galilee. Nazareth and Cana were cities thought to be within this territory. (Joshua 19:10-16)

ZIDON See Sidon.

ZIKLAG A city in the southern part of Judah. (Joshua 15:31) It was assigned to the tribe of Simeon. (Joshua 19:5; I Chronicles 4:30) Achish, king of Gath, gave the city to David when he was fleeing from Saul. (I Samuel 27:5-7) It was plundered by the Amalekites but David recovered the spoils and distributed them among many towns. (I Samuel 30:1-31) Here also David received the news of Saul's death. (II Samuel 1:1-4; 4:10) It was inhabited after the captivity. (Nehemiah 11:28)

ZIN A wilderness south of Palestine through which the children of Israel passed on their way to Canaan. It was from here that the spies were sent out to explore the land of Canaan. (Num. 13:21) Kadesh-barnea was located within its limits. (Num. 20:1)

ZION (also Sion) It was one of the hills on which Jerusalem stood. In the O. T. it is mentioned as the seat of a Jebusite fortress. When David captured it, he changed the name to the City of David. (II Samuel 5:7; I Chronicles 11:5) He brought the Ark of the Covenant here, and from that time it became sacred. (II Samuel 6:10-12) The term Zion is frequently used to designate all of Jerusalem. (II Kings 19:21; Psalms 48, 69:35, 133:3; Isaiah 1:8, 3:16, 4:3)

ZOAR A small town in the Jordan valley to which Lot fled when Sodom and Gomorrah were destroyed. (Genesis 19:20-25) Lot and his daughters dwelt in a cave near Zoar. (Genesis 19:30)

ZORAH A town in Judah inhabited by the children of Dan. (Joshua 19:41; Judges 18:2) It was the birthplace of Samson and also where he was buried. (Judges 13:2,25; 16:31)

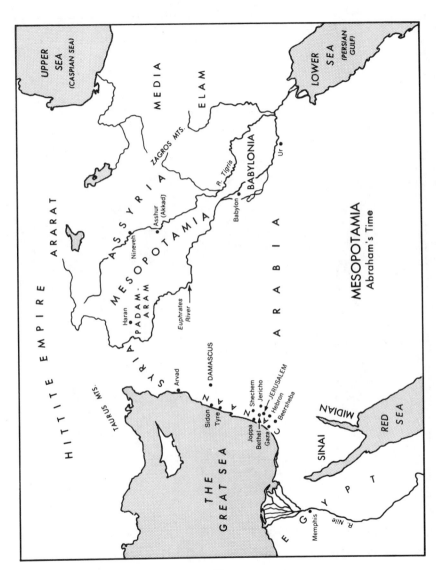

UPPER SEA (CASPIAN SEA)

LOWER SEA (PERSIAN GULF)

MEDIA

ELAM

ARARAT

ZAGROS MTS.

R. Tigris

Ur

ASSYRIA

BABYLONIA

Asshur (Akkad)

Babylon

Nineveh

MESOPOTAMIA

PADAM-ARAM

Haran

Euphrates River

MESOPOTAMIA
Abraham's Time

HITTITE EMPIRE

ARABIA

TAURUS MTS.

SYRIA

Arvad

DAMASCUS

Sidon

Tyre

Shechem

Jericho

JERUSALEM

Hebron

Beersheba

Joppa

Bethel

Gaza

MIDIAN

SINAI

RED SEA

THE GREAT SEA

EGYPT

Memphis

R. Nile

63

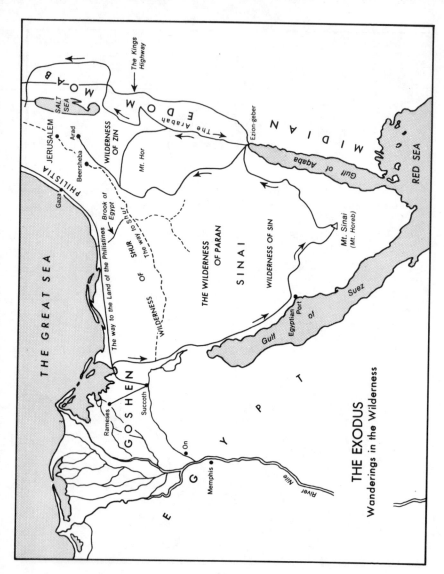

THE EXODUS
Wanderings in the Wilderness

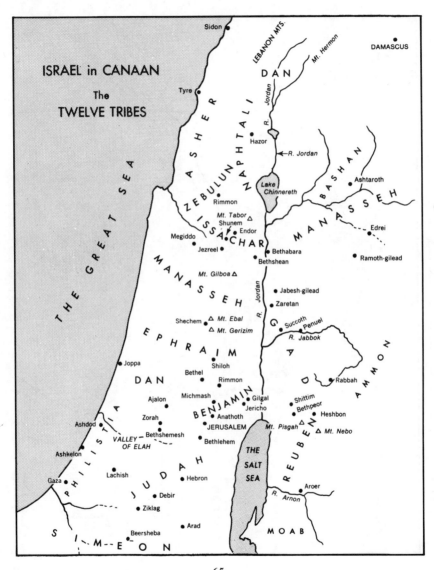

ISRAEL in CANAAN

The
TWELVE TRIBES

DAMASCUS

Sidon

LEBANON MTS.

Mt. Hermon

DAN

Tyre

R. Jordan

A
S
H
E
R

N
A
P
H
T
A
L
I

Hazor

←R. Jordan

Lake
Chinnereth

ASHTAROTH

Ashtaroth

ZEBULUN

B
A
S
H
A
N

M
A
N
A
S
S
E
H

Rimmon

Mt. Tabor △
Shunem

ISSA•CHAR

Endor

Edrei

Megiddo

Jezreel

Bethabara

Bethshean

Ramoth-gilead

M
A
N
A
S
S
E
H

Mt. Gilboa △

R. Jordan

Jabesh-gilead

Zaretan

E
P
H
R
A
I
M

Shechem   △ Mt. Ebal
           △ Mt. Gerizim

Succoth
Penuel

R. Jabbok

G
A
D

Joppa

Shiloh

DAN

Bethel

Rimmon

Rabbah

A
M
M
O
N

Ajalon

Michmash

Gilgal

Shittim

BENJAMIN

Jericho

Bethpeor

Heshbon

Zorah

Anathoth

JERUSALEM

Ashdod

Bethshemesh

Bethlehem

Mt. Pisgah △

△ Mt. Nebo

P
H
I
L
I
S
T
I
A

VALLEY
OF ELAH

THE
SALT
SEA

R
E
U
B
E
N

Ashkelon

Gaza

Lachish

J
U
D
A
H

Hebron

Aroer

Debir

R. Arnon

Ziklag

Arad

S
I
M
E
O
N

Beersheba

MOAB

THE   GREAT   SEA

65

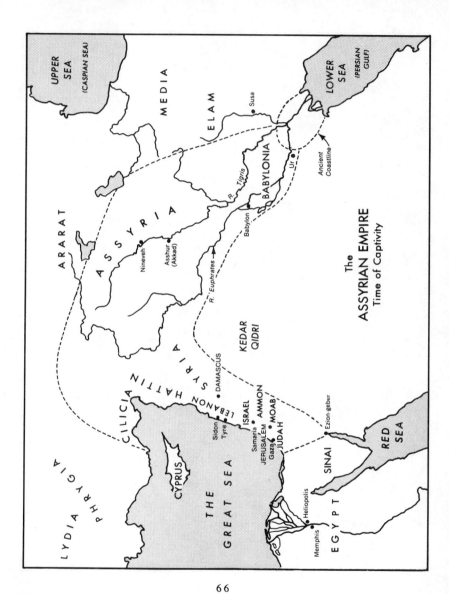

The

ASSYRIAN EMPIRE
Time of Captivity

UPPER SEA (CASPIAN SEA)

LOWER SEA (PERSIAN GULF)

MEDIA

ELAM

Susa

Ancient Coastline

ARARAT

R. Tigris

BABYLONIA

Ur

ASSYRIA

Nineveh

Asshur (Akkad)

Babylon

R. Euphrates

KEDAR
QIDRI

SYRIA

DAMASCUS

CILICIA

LEBANON

HATTIN

Sidon

Tyre

ISRAEL
AMMON
Samaria
MOAB
JERUSALEM
Gaza
JUDAH

Ezion-geber

RED
SEA

CYPRUS

SINAI

LYDIA

PHRYGIA

THE
GREAT SEA

Heliopolis

EGYPT

Memphis

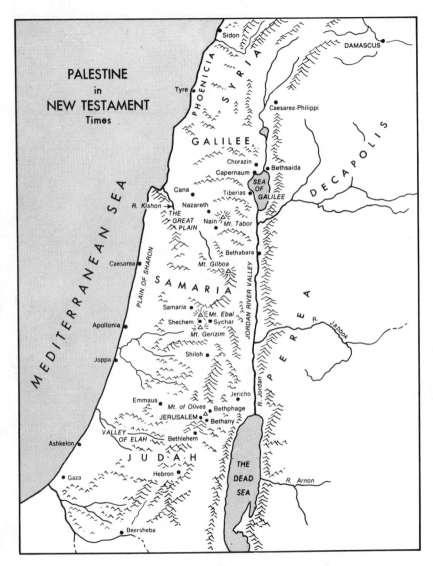

PALESTINE
in
NEW TESTAMENT
Times

MEDITERRANEAN SEA

PHOENICIA

SYRIA

Sidon

DAMASCUS

Tyre

Caesarea-Philippi

GALILEE

DECAPOLIS

Chorazin

Capernaum

Bethsaida

Cana

Tiberias

SEA OF GALILEE

R. Kishon →

THE GREAT PLAIN

Nazareth

Nain

Mt. Tabor

Caesarea

PLAIN OF SHARON

Bethabara

Mt. Gilboa

SAMARIA

JORDAN RIVER VALLEY

Samaria

Mt. Ebal

Apollonia

Shechem

Sychar

Mt. Gerizim

P E R E A

R. Jabbok

Shiloh

Joppa

Jericho

Emmaus

Mt. of Olives

Bethphage

JERUSALEM

Bethany

R. Jordan

Ashkelon

VALLEY OF ELAH

Bethlehem

Gaza

J U D A H

Hebron

THE DEAD SEA

R. Arnon

Beersheba

PAUL'S MISSIONARY JOURNEYS

Paul's First Missionary Journey . . . .
    Acts 13 & 14 . . . Early 47 A.D.—Fall of 49 A.D.

Paul's Second Missionary Journey ._._._._._.
    Acts 15:40 to Acts 18:22
    Spring 51 A. D.—Spring 53 A. D.

Paul's Third Missionary Journey _ _ _ _ _ _ _ _
    Acts 18:23 to Acts 21:17
    Fall of 53 A. D.—May 57 A. D.

Paul's Journey to Rome _____
    Acts 27 & 28 . . . Fall of 59 A. D.—60 A. D.

a. Cities visited by Paul engraved thus: ANTIOCH
b. Other cities not visited by him thus: Colossae
c. Locations of Seven Churches mentioned
    in Revelations engraved as follows
    with star preceding name: ★ Laodicea

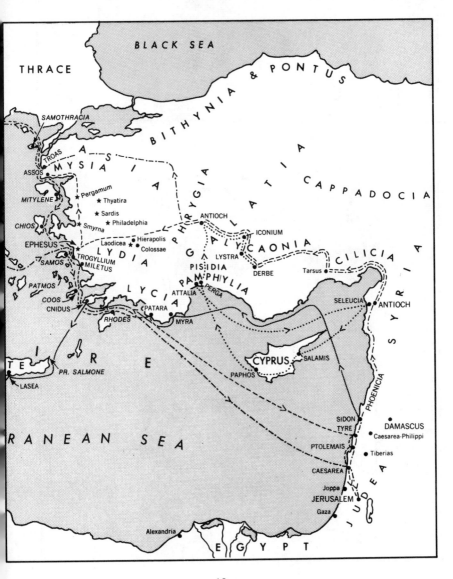

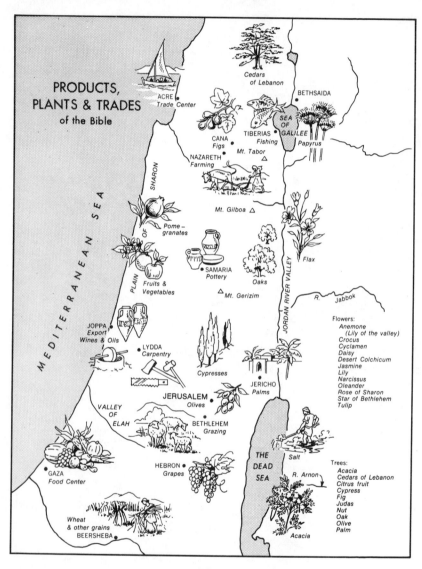

PRODUCTS,
PLANTS & TRADES
of the Bible

Cedars
of Lebanon

ACRE
Trade Center

BETHSAIDA

SEA
OF
GALILEE

CANA
Figs

TIBERIAS
Fishing

Papyrus

NAZARETH
Farming

Mt. Tabor △

SHARON

Mt. Gilboa △

PLAIN OF

Pome-
granates

Flax

JORDAN RIVER VALLEY

MEDITERRANEAN SEA

SAMARIA
Pottery

Oaks

Fruits &
Vegetables

△ Mt. Gerizim

R.   Jabbok

Flowers:
    Anemone
      (Lily of the valley)
    Crocus
    Cyclamen
    Daisy
    Desert Colchicum
    Jasmine
    Lily
    Narcissus
    Oleander
    Rose of Sharon
    Star of Bethlehem
    Tulip

JOPPA
Export
Wines & Oils

LYDDA
Carpentry

Cypresses

JERICHO
Palms

JERUSALEM
Olives

VALLEY
OF
ELAH

BETHLEHEM
Grazing

THE
DEAD
SEA

Salt

R. Arnon

Trees:
    Acacia
    Cedars of Lebanon
    Citrus fruit
    Cypress
    Fig
    Judas
    Nut
    Oak
    Olive
    Palm

GAZA
Food Center

HEBRON
Grapes

Wheat
& other grains
BEERSHEBA

Acacia

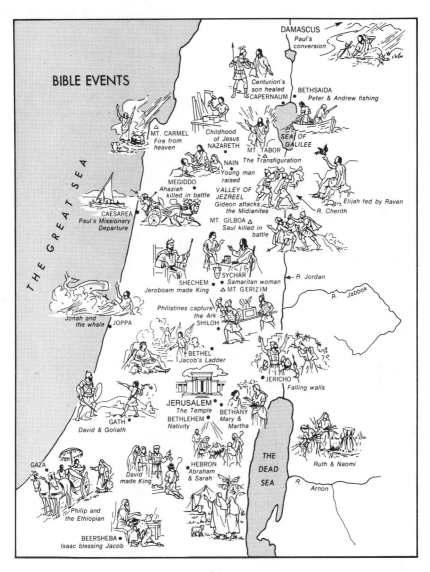

BIBLE EVENTS

DAMASCUS
Paul's conversion

Centurion's son healed
CAPERNAUM

BETHSAIDA
Peter & Andrew fishing

MT. CARMEL
Fire from heaven

Childhood of Jesus
NAZARETH

SEA OF GALILEE

MT. TABOR
The Transfiguration

NAIN
Young man raised

MEGIDDO
Ahaziah killed in battle

VALLEY OF JEZREEL
Gideon attacks the Midianites

Elijah fed by Raven

R. Cherith

THE GREAT SEA

CAESAREA
Paul's Missionary Departure

MT. GILBOA
Saul killed in battle

SHECHEM
Jeroboam made King

SYCHAR
Samaritan woman
MT. GERIZIM

R. Jordan

R. Jabbok

Philistines capture the Ark
SHILOH

Jonah and the whale
JOPPA

BETHEL
Jacob's Ladder

JERICHO
Falling walls

JERUSALEM
The Temple
BETHLEHEM
Nativity

BETHANY
Mary & Martha

GATH
David & Goliath

GAZA

David made King

HEBRON
Abraham & Sarah

THE DEAD SEA

R. Arnon

Ruth & Naomi

Philip and the Ethiopian

BEERSHEBA
Isaac blessing Jacob

71